SO...
YOU SAY YOU WANT TO
SING

MEMOIRS OF A BACKGROUND VOCALIST

ANGELA PRIMM

For permission requests, write to the author, addressed
"Attention: Permissions " to angela@angelaprimm.com

Angela Primm Ministries
c/o Valencia Houston, Administrator
(615) 974-7200
angela@angelaprimm.com
www.angelaprimm.com

Ordering Information:
For details, visit www.angelaprimm.com

Print ISBN: 978-1-7368412-0-4
eBook ISBN: 978-1-7368412-1-1

Editor: Kaitlyn Calcote

Master Editor: Nancy Thomas Rozier

Cover Design & Interior Layout: Brian Wooten, Brikwoo Creative Group, LLC.

Photography: Padrion Scott, Sr., P. Scott Photography

Printed in the United States of America.

First Edition

CONTENTS

DEDICATION

My book-and indeed, my life story-is dedicated to all the artists, singers, instrumentalists, producers, writers, music directors, pastors and churches who have embraced my gifting, and thus made it possible to develop into my career. Without your embrace, my gifting could never have been utilized in such a blessed way. Your inclusiveness became my welcomed journey of which I write. Thank you all for loving me!

ACKNOWLEDGMENTS

Please allow me first to acknowledge my husband, John Primm. He so graciously allows me the time to get work done, that is singing and now writing. Without his patience and love, this would be a tiring and unwelcomed task. He never questions my activities; he only asks, "what's for dinner?" I love you, John Primm.

I want to acknowledge the courage of my youngest editor and spiritual daughter, Kaitlyn Calcote. She took this manuscript and made it her priority to get it done. She dismantled all fear, uncertainty, and doubt of accomplishing such a work. Your labor is not in vain, Sweetheart. You have convinced me as a writer. I trust and thank you. As you say, "Next book, Mommy?"

Needing additional proofing, opinions, and advice from a prayer warrior, I solicited the service of my other spiritual daughter, Elder Jocelyn Hill. She jumped right in with both feet and "eagle eyes" and got it done! Thank you, my Baby! I appreciate you more than you'll ever know.

Lastly, to acknowledge the professionalism of my final editor, Sis. Nancy Rozier. She shared her gift in editing and creating word pictures; she changed, rearranged, and corrected all that was necessary in making this piece of work enjoyable and palatable for all readers. Both her suggestions and questions rendered eye openers for additional clarity to subjects. What a wonderful and enlightening experience it was to work with you! Until next time…I hope!!! LOL!

FOREWORD
By Geron Davis

I love to read. I have read, and own, literally hundreds of books, including many self-help books. Occasionally, I'll get a book, about a subject, written by someone who doesn't actually know a thing they're writing about. (i.e. don't write a book on raising kids, if you don't actually have any) The book you're holding is NOT that kind of book. I have had the privilege of working with my phenomenal friend, Angela Primm, in many recording sessions, for over two decades. I have also had the blessing of working with her in many concerts, and "live worship" settings.

When given the opportunity to minister, Angie (what I call her), has a style, and anointing, uniquely her own . . . and it's full throttle! The difference in Angie, and some singers I've met, is that, when someone else is in charge, whether it's a session or a service, she adapts to that setting. With zero attitude. She has done black gospel, country, high church choral, pop, southern gospel, and even kid's choir music! She is always professional, and adaptive, when it's her time to follow. Which, in my opinion, qualifies her to be a leader.

Her decades of experience, including singing on dozens of award winning projects, (including Dove, Grammy, CMA, and SGMA award winners... just to name a few), has earned her tons of information, that has made her better – and, now, can make YOU better!

So GET READY... get a highlighter, and a notepad; GET SET... turn the rest of the world "off" for a little bit ...and GO!

You're about to discover what we already know, that spending time with Angie is always an adventure!!

INTRODUCTION

Me, a background vocalist (BGV)? Who would have thought that this would be a career for me or anyone? Who knew? It's nothing I ever heard of or aspired to be. My work history since high school was that of a banker. I have been asked on *sooo* many occasions, "How did you get started in the music business as a background singer?" "How do you recommend me getting started?" And "Can you train my child to do what you do?"

Singing has been a life journey for me. My musical training has derived from experience. God has been the controller of every aspect of my life that has allowed such a career to materialize. He has orchestrated every opportunity I have had in singing, both good and not so good. He has allowed the good to encourage me and the "not so good" to teach me. I'm *sooo* honored that He has chosen to give me a gift that encourages and allows people to feel His love. It's not a gift that I own or asked for, but one that is borrowed from Him, and I'm obligated and endowed to use this gift for His glory to serve all people.

Singing is a gift that can easily cause one to puff up and become prideful. This particular talent causes people to embrace you, celebrate you, and desire you. If you are not careful, you can easily believe that it was really your idea to bless yourself with the gift and that it's you they love and worship and not the Creator of the gift. People are always prone to celebrate the house and not the builder of it. They will celebrate and admonish the gift but fail to recognize the Giver of the gift. Yes, the Lucifer syndrome is yet alive!

Humbleness and humility are the antidotes for such a syndrome. Through prayer, He will guide you around this monster that continues to demand your thoughts of your greatness for its food. Those who suffer from this disease will find themselves alone, uninvited and wondering "Where did the crowd go?" "What happened to me being a god?" "It was me they really loved, right?" "The song I sang was best." "Did they not stand and applaud for me?" "Where is the red carpet for me?" "I'm entitled to recognition." "Was not the applause greater for me?" "Where is my pat-on-the-back?" "Why are they not standing when I enter a room?" When Lucifer ended up with only a third of the angels, I'm sure he was wondering, "How did this happen?"

A singer must stay focused on the task at hand. 1 Timothy 4:14-16 (TPT) says, *"Don't minimize the powerful gift that operates in your life, for it was imparted to you by the laying on of hands of the elders and was activated through the prophecy they spoke over you. Make all of this your constant meditation and make it real with your life so everyone can see that you are moving forward. Give careful attention to your spiritual life and every cherished truth you teach, for living what you preach will then release even more abundant life inside you and to all those who listen to you."* How profound! Singers, this is written to us! We must remember, though we use our gifting well, it is the Lord who provides the gift, and He opens and closes doors. He is in control. He will launch you into religious and secular ministering opportunities if you remain pliable to His will.

Remember that God is always at work! Join Him! Obeying His Word and acting as He instructs, in a Kingdom way, pays. However, exemplifying the seeds of Lucifer and compromising integrity so that your gift is heard, used, and glorified, does not. "Obedience is better than sacrifice" (1 Samuel 15:22 NLT).

Understand and KNOW that God has a plan for you. He really does! It is our responsibility to seek Him and trust Him to reveal our journey daily. It's really true…. This is His world and we are in it! Our lives woven together create one huge tapestry for Him that He cherishes. He cherished it so much that He chose to come and die for us, that the tapestry would return to the right hands—His. We are all a part of His plan; let us use our gift accordingly. In doing so, you will maximize your life on earth and set up timber for the New Earth!

I strongly recommend anyone with a gift or talent to submit yourself to higher learning. Please understand that not everyone will have professional training for various reasons, but their gift has made room for them. Higher learning will not be available to all. Circumstances will arise and your gift may be needed now! Then give it the best you have. Submit your two fish and five loaves of bread and simply watch God move. However, do not negate the fact that there are schools in place to assist your gift with abilities you have never imagined. Believe it or not, the world of music is highly structured.

There are various forums where professional knowledge is required. But for me, not aspiring to be a singer growing up, I didn't desire to learn it. I only did it! Life, by way of experience, has been my teacher. When the need arose for a singer and I was there, I did all I could to glorify God with His gift to me.

All of my accomplishments are made by God's favor. Every single one! My living has been made by God nudging men's hearts to ask me to sing. Nothing complicated, only God's will being done. I learned that God decides what He desires for you to do. You decide your obedience. And this has been true for me. God would place on men's hearts to have Angela Primm sing on their project. They call and say, "On this song, we want you to add that soulful thing that you're known for," and at that point, I'm hired! Nothing super spiritual, complicated, or jumping through hoops.

My livelihood has depended solely on God's favor, just that simple. Thank You Jesus for Your provision. It has been a process, a lifelong, yet continual, process, and this is how it all began. This is why I sing....

CHAPTER 1
BACKGROUND VOCALIST IN THE MAKING

The Yellow Bird Sings

Oscarretta Hewlett, my mommy, *(Yes, that is her name. No one could make that up!)* was the singer of the family. Everything and everyone around her sang. You sang when you were happy, you sang when you were sad, you sang when you were sick, and you sang when you were well. Every occasion rendered a need for a song. Well, at the age of 42, my mother battled diabetes, high blood pressure, narcolepsy, and degenerative heart disease. Even though all these ailments were present within her body, she felt a new discomfort in her abdomen area that she couldn't explain. Something was growing and making her nauseous daily! Knowing that her pregnancy days were gone, she knew something was very wrong. She tried explaining this to my father who repeatedly told her she was taking too many medications.

Mommy made an appointment with our family doctor, Dr. Cole. After running tests, he sadly informed her that they did find a cancerous tumor in her abdomen. He explained that the only treatment available for that type of cancer was chemotherapy. He explained that the harshness of this treatment could affect her other ailments and its prescribed medications. There were definitely risks involved. The treatment for this type of cancer was a long and dangerous process. Encouraged by family to live, Mommy took her first treatment, but it didn't take a scientist to know that the tumor was still growing. She knew the chemo had not stopped the growth. After a two-week trial, Mommy returned to the doctor's office to hear the report that she already knew—the chemo did not work. With a somber face, the doctor instead informed her that the tumor had actually grown.

While Mommy was coming to grips with this news and contemplating how to tell the family, there was a knock on the door and then entered an intern. He asked Dr. Cole to please allow him a moment to speak with him. The doctor explained that his visit with Mrs. Hewlett was just about over, and that he would be with him shortly. However, the intern insisted on speaking to the doctor immediately, as the matter was concerning Mrs. Hewlett.

The doctor left and returned within two minutes. When recounting the story, Mommy always said, "Now you know my eyes are big, but his eyes were larger than mine and any white man's I'd ever seen!"
He said, "Mrs. Hewlett!"
She said, "What?!"
He said, "You're pregnant!"
She said, "Cancer I can believe, but not pregnant!"

The doctor recommended a legal abortion due to the chemo that had already been administered. He explained that the exposure to chemo would render the baby either a living vegetable or extremely retarded *(to which my husband* now remarks: *"One out of two isn't bad!"*). The doctor allowed her two weeks to decide on the abortion. Mommy was a firm believer against abortion and was deeply troubled. When she told my sister about the baby, she said all Joan could say was, "Mother!!! Are you still carrying on like that?!" Mommy said she couldn't deny it because she had a belly full!

The night before she had to give the doctor her decision about the abortion, she had a dream. She said in her dream she was sitting on the porch. In the corner of this porch was a huge, ornate bird cage that contained the fattest yellow bird she had ever seen. The fat bird was swinging and singing *sooo* loudly that it was rude! It was too loud to enjoy!

My sister, Joan, called the next day to get a report, and my mother told her about her dream. Joan began to scream, "Mother, Mother, whatever you do, don't kill it! Whatever it is, it's going to sing! Mother, that fat yellow bird is singing! That baby is going to sing!"

Mommy had already decided against abortion, though she was concerned about her ability to raise the child because she was so sickly. The doctor advised against her having a child in her condition. Graciously, Joan agreed to raise the child if something happened to Mommy. *(Thank You, Father God, for the miracle of my Mommy! She lived to raise me 18 years! That's another story!)*

Mommy was on bedrest the last six weeks of her pregnancy. Due to complications, she had to carry me for ten months *(My lateness began in the womb, so don't judge me!)* Back in those days when babies were delivered, doctors would spank them on their bottoms to clear their lungs *(today spanking on the bottom will send you to jail!)*. She said,

"When they spanked you, you released the loudest cry I had ever heard from any of my children! I knew then, yep, that's that Fat Yellow Bird!"

My Singing Childhood

My career started as a little girl who laid down and woke up listening to music on a beige and white portable handheld record player. I would keep it plugged in beside my bed and listen, listen, listen *sooo* intently to the various parts that were sung in a song; that is called harmony.

It was like a jigsaw puzzle to me, to be able to hear the various parts singers would use to create a wonderful sound. It was amazing!!! I would choose a part in a song and the challenge was to follow this part to the end. Then I would "join" the group and rehearse with them every day. *(I would; just ask my dresser mirror!)* When someone would mess up and miss their part, we would have to start from the beginning of the song again until everyone got it right. I'd lift the needle on the player and start it again!

My sisters, Joan and Diana, were *sooo* instrumental in training my ear to hear. Joan was the oldest. Before I was born, she had a career in music. The most famous person she sang with was James Brown, the "I Feel Good – da da da da da da da – like I knew that I would" guy. It seemed to me that when I was born, she was there waiting to tell me what to do, and I DID IT!

Joan was the disciplinarian of the family. You did what she said and she didn't settle for "I don't feel like singing." You SANG when she was in town! I'd often say under my breath, *"Whatever Joan! You ain't my momma!" (LOL!)* She would gather the girls (Diana, Meridith, who is Joan's daughter, my mother, and me) around her upright piano and make us sing.

Word pronunciation was her pet peeve. "Pronounce your words," she'd say. "Don't get all excited with a chord so that you are no longer speaking English!" I must say, she was not Pentecostal! *(LOL!)* And she wasn't having anything less than the best in any musical presentation. This requirement was for us and the community.

Joan disciplined our community with music. Parents loved her! She would collect the neighborhood children once a week and take them to choir rehearsal and make them sing. Then on Sunday, the families would come to support and witness the hard work of the children. On Joan's part, this was a good evangelistic strategy. Kids respect discipline and love the end result of their hard work. They loved Joan, and as strict as she was, they knew she loved them. She would even book this choir to sing Sunday afternoons at various church programs in and around the city of Indianapolis, Indiana.

We were always busy singing. I remember Joan had a car with bad brakes and a hole in the bottom, and the guys would stick their feet through the hole to help the car stop! Sparks would fly everywhere, but we were going to church and we were going to get there "safe" in Jesus' name. *(LOL!)*

She was such a disciplinarian that she could control the children with a look. One night, while they were rehearsing, a lady who had been drinking stumbled in off the street to ask if she could sing for some money. The kids began to giggle, and Joan gave them "the eye" and it stopped immediately. Diana, who was the pianist, was saved by the piano covering her face.

Joan couldn't see her tears of laughter streaming as the lady sang, "Ring Them Bells" with an operatic sound, mixed with alcohol!

Joan, while dealing with an alcohol addiction herself, heard the impaired talent and gave her an offering, which the lady thought should have been more, causing her to complain loudly. Joan dared the kids to laugh and made them sit, astute and respectful, to allow the lady to leave with dignity. As soon as the lady cleared the building, choir rehearsal was OVER!!! Camp broke; all you could see were children making a beeline across the street to the church's neighborhood store to let it out. They laid out in the floor holding their bellies, crying with laughter!

Diana was not a disciplinarian. She always made singing and life fun. Her approach to singing was completely different. She would ask you to join her in singing and challenge you to figure it out. Diana made singing a game. We would sit on the front porch and figure out a part to sing and try to be the first to get to the end of the song successfully. It was fun!

I love being in her company yet today! She is so gentle and attentive. Her spirit soars with love and precision for music. We would hear a chord or harmony and race to be the first to catch it, vocally. It was *sooo* much fun. And we would dare each other to be the first to try it out on Mommy.

Our mother was one who didn't go for a lot of your vocal licks and runs. Now if it happened while singing, that was different. But you were not going to rehearse the Holy Spirit; that was blasphemous to her!!!

Diana and I would sneak in a chord while Mommy would be rehearsing her part, passionately, with her eyes closed, only to see an eye lift open to look at us as if to say, "Now what was that?" We would be *sooo* tickled, but never laughed about it out loud. That was our secret way of introducing Mommy to something "cool." We knew if we kept repeating it the same way, she would think it was a proper part of the song.

When Diana married and moved out of the house, her training didn't end. We would go to her house and practice using the broom and mop handles for our mics. We would become Shirley Caesar, Albertina Walker, The Caravans, James Cleveland Choir, and even The Jackson 5! We would practice dance steps and have concerts on her front porch singing along with the records. We convinced ourselves that we had a packed audience and would sing our hearts out! We'd make costumes out of towels, house dresses, and sheets. Hilarious, but true! And, of course, the fight would always be who gets to be Michael Jackson this time! We would trip all over each other trying to "moon walk!"

Meridith (MiMi) was the one who taught me courage and boldness. To my knowledge, she never feared anything. To this day, I believe she would walk through a ring of fire, though she's the smallest of us all. *(Diana, I wonder if MiMi suffered from short-man's syndrome? LOL!)* Boy, she'd take any challenge by the throat! This boldness was transferred to her singing abilities. If you want the message in the song to be loud and clear, get MiMi to lead it. There would be no doubt that you heard and understood everything she said! Just in case you didn't get it the first time, MiMi was known for repeating her entire song.

MiMi was a born leader. Under her lead, you'd do it right, which could mean over and over again until it was right. She was definitely Joan's daughter! Everything I was afraid to say to Joan, I'd say to her! *Oooh*, she would work my nerves! I remember just wanting her to be quiet. She was, by default, my punching bag. But don't misunderstand me; she held her own. I knew she was older, and I respected her to some degree, even though I was "Auntie." Let's just say I knew how far to go.

MiMi was meticulous about my appearance. She has always been about presentation. Clothes had to fit correctly. Underclothes were just as important as outer garments. She insisted, and it's true, that how your underclothes form you determines how your outer garments show you. Even today, while living hundreds of miles away from each other, when we come together, we always have something in common, such as the same pair of shoes. It never fails! Ladies ask me all the time, "Where do you get your jewelry?" I get it from her. She sends me jewelry and I make my clothes to match!

Now, young ladies don't even know what "slips" are. Shame on us older women, for we dropped the ball in training our ladies and have been dropping modesty ever since. We simply show too much unguarded! When did gospel music become sexy? Okay, that's another book! But with MiMi's training, I was not afraid to grace a stage.

Oscarretta Hewlett
My mother is the legend for me, hands down. She was born February 5, 1918 and only acquired a third-grade education. Although she endured *sooo* many oppositions in life,

she taught us to strive and not be bitter about circumstances that we could not control, but to roll with the punches. She'd say, "Never give up!" "Make your message clear!" "Your words are all you have, so use them wisely." "Mean your message."

Mommy was a perfectionist with her girls and guarded us with her life. She guarded our appearance, and everything we wore had to meet her approval. At an early age, in a gentle, yet firm, way, she made it clear to us how a lady was to carry herself and look a certain way. Anything contrary to her standards was unacceptable.

Mommy and Angie with ruffled pantaloons

Having very little money, she would get material and make us clothes that would enable us to have dignity, if nothing else. She was a seamstress, and so are her girls. She was a singer, and so are her girls. She was a minister, and so are her girls. She poured her life into us and made sure we got it. I hated sewing with her and hated when she knew I was sewing. She would inspect the garment and pull it apart if it was not done right, only to instruct me on how to do it correctly. Some garments would escape her eagle eye, but only until it was time to wear it. The lopsidedness spoke loud and clear that Mommy didn't get a hold of that piece! *(LOL!)* She not only guarded what we wore, but what we heard.

There was some music that was just not welcome in her home; however, we did have friends whose homes were less confining. Even some gospel music was scrutinized and considered "too far, too worldly." Her favorite phrase was, "Whatcha listening to, baby?" She would say it carelessly walking by, not as a question, but a gesture to let you know that she was listening. She heard *everything*!

My mother disciplined with her emotion of love. You loved her *sooo* much that you didn't want to do anything to disappoint her. You must know that I was the sickly child, the *oops* baby that knew how to push her buttons. I knew how to work the system, which would often infuriate MiMi who was closest to my age and knew what I was doing! MiMi always made sure Mommy "knew" what I was doing. She always had a way of bringing to Mommy's attention that I was misbehaving. *(For real, MiMi?! Could someone please bring me the duct tape for her loud mouth?!)* MiMi talked too much!

Mommy

Joan, Diana, Gary, and MiMi

Mothers and Daughters Gospel Group

Mommy always made sure to be a part of anything musical in church. She loved the church and anything to do with it, and since her gift to the body was music, she never hesitated to do her part. She loved working with her gift in the church. While being a Sunday school teacher, an usher, and choir member (mass choir and ladies chorus), Mommy formed a group and called it the Mothers and Daughters Gospel Group.

Mommy's singing group was compiled of mothers and daughters (biological and spiritual) who desired to minister in music together as family. Understand that the young girls, like myself, were there because their mothers told them to be—I'm just saying! We would have rather been somewhere playing jacks or tag football! Back then, mothers decided what was best for their children, and not the children telling them what to do. Therefore, our afternoons were spent preparing for the next engagement, rehearsing. (Ughhh!)

Mommy and Aunt Lula in women's choir

Mothers and Daughters Singing Group

We traveled around Indiana singing with Diana as the pianist, wearing the black and white uniforms Mommy made, which consisted of long black skirts, ruffled white blouses, and black patent leather shoes. The group was well and widely received, and everyone dearly called her "Gra-Mommy." To be her child, blood related or not, you were going to sing.

Understanding the responsibility of singing, rehearsing, and having to be a part of various programs all the time was not something I wanted to do growing up, but I had to because I lived with my mother. But man, I often day-dreamed of the time when I would be old enough to get out of her house!

I didn't desire singing. I would express the lack of this desire to my mother quite often and her response would be, "You're not old enough to know what you want. I'm your mother; therefore, I will tell you what you want and you're going to do it." Wow…it was just that simple. Sometimes pouting, defiant, and rebellious, I had to sing, and she didn't take into consideration not one moment what I wanted. She was mother and she made my choice for me!

Sometimes people would request me to sing a particular song that I led, and she wouldn't allow me to lead if I was "cutting up" or had misbehaved that day or week. She would simply respond "Oh, thank you for your request, but Angela is not prepared to lead this song today." I would ask, "Mommy, why can't I sing it? We know it." She told me, "You did not conduct yourself according to the words of that song this week, and you're not going to be singing a lie on my watch, no ma'am!" That would be the end of that.

Diana would get so frustrated with me because she loved me *sooo* much and didn't understand why I was so contrary. She would say, "Angie, just behave and obey Mommy. You know how she is! Just behave!" But me, I always had to push buttons. *Ughhh*; I was terrible!!! Sometimes in the pictures you could see me pouting and not wanting to be there. My shoulders would be lifted higher than my chin in defiance. It was awful. But my mother cared not one moment about it. She knew she was the mother and I was going to do as she said.

Going Solo

Because my mother traveled around the city singing, a church would recognize me in their audience as one of her daughters and did not hesitate to ask me to render a selection in their service. This is how my gifting assignments began. If nothing more than, "I understand that Sis. Angie is in the house and we'd like to impose upon her to render us an "A" selection if she would." *FOR REAL*?! I just knew that I had left Joan and Mommy at home! Why are they asking me to sing? *Ughhh*!

I would go visit my high school friends' homes and their parents would ask, "Aren't you Mrs. Hewlett's daughter who sings?" My friends would answer before I could come up with a, "Not really." They would leap forward with a, "Yes, she is! Ask her to sing something because she won't sing for us." I wouldn't sing for them or me! I didn't want to. Would somebody please turn off this "sing" button?

For an easy credit in high school, guess what I did. I joined the high school choir. Let it be known that it was my most problematic class. My teacher hated me! He hated my sound. It was not a sound he desired for his high school choir. He was so mean to me that it caused my mother to come and have a sit-down meeting with him. She knew his frustration was the sound of a black singer fitting into a white choir. She understood it all too well; blackness had its place, and it wasn't in a white choir. Mommy was all too familiar with this uphill battle. She knew that if navigated correctly, it would build character in me, and this would help prepare me for life and its struggles as a black person.

She watched me very carefully to make sure nothing crossed the line between my teacher and me and insisted that

I be polite, yet determined. It was a challenging, frustrating, heartbreaking class. I wanted him to like me as other teachers did. He tried to get me to quit his all-white choir by mistreating me, but it did not work. I wasn't giving up that easily. I needed the credit; he didn't. I passed his class with flying colors after my mother's involvement in the pursuit of fair treatment toward me. He knew that she was asking questions and he had better have the right answers.

Leaving Home

At the age of eighteen and right after graduation, I married my high school sweetheart, Wayne Wright, who had just joined the Army. At this point, becoming a military wife and leaving Indiana catapulted my singing assignments worldwide. Every military post we were stationed at needed a singer in their chapel.

In the military, fellowship was precious and personal. The military wives would always come together for prayer and support. I loved the mothering and mentoring I received while stationed in Ft. Knox, Kentucky, from both my pastor and his wife, affectionately known as "Big Daddy and Big Momma." They were our parents in the faith. Some of us, as myself, had just left home and military living was brand new, as was marriage! They took us under their wings and guided us through life with prayer, love, and Bible studies.

There was always a need for singing every time we gathered. I was the one appointed to lead the meetings off in song. We would pray until something happened. Even when we, the younger wives, thought we were done, the older mothers would come and coach us into praying more for the breakthrough we needed, or they thought we needed! Singing and praying could sometimes last all night!

I always wanted to serve the church, and singing was the best service I could provide for growing churches *(which is what they'd tell me)*. With my desire to serve God's people, it became my job by default. The most developed gift I had to give was my voice, whether soloist, group, or leading a choir.

You better believe I started seeking other avenues of service for the church. I was not going to be just a singer. No!!! Can I be the Sunday School teacher or something? I can teach—watch this! But God! "Sis. Angie, Pastor is the guest preacher at a church down the road and he'd like you to accompany him with a song, are you available?" What could I say if I was available? No, I'd rather teach Sunday school?! So, there I was, preparing for the evening's assignment…singing.

Then other pastors would call my pastor and ask if I could sing for them at their upcoming program. I'd tell Pastor to tell them NO, but I would gladly sew a dress for their wife or teach a Sunday School class! Pastor would send me on because the community needed a voice of encouragement, and he knew of my God-given desire to serve. Needless to say, Pastor began to send me out regularly to special events to represent the church. *(Uh, Pastor, was this a form of pimping? I'm just asking, that's all! LOL!)*

God's gift began to make room for me with people I didn't know. A song was needed to bridge a gap by way of church, family gatherings, community efforts, and even official military functions. I was always called and available. Someone always needed a song somewhere!

Because of my deep desire to serve and be a blessing to

people, I was content with being the military wife who sung. This gift would bring cultures together. Singing would tear down racial, financial, and spiritual barriers that are in and out of the church. God used a song, even one that I'd sing, to accomplish life-changing events. He still does it! I never wanted to interfere with that. Never! I'd have to tell my flesh to go sit down somewhere!!! This is God's doing and it's marvelous. *(But God, is there a need for a Sunday School teacher somewhere? I'm just asking!)*

Ft. Campbell, KY/Nashville, TN

We received military orders to move from Ft. Knox to Bremerhaven, Germany. We were stationed there for three years, and while there, I sang my heart out for the morale of soldiers away from home. It just so happened that church members from Ft. Knox were also stationed in our area and the feeling of family was within reach. We had us some good old-fashioned church every Sunday!

Funny story: My church family would meet at our pastor's house after Sunday's church service to eat, play games, and watch current shows or videos sent from the States. American television networks in Germany were always six months behind. My husband had a connection for getting the best current videos, and I couldn't wait to share them with others! I had no idea that he had begun to circulate porn. He was selling pornography videos illegally and had to mask them with different legal titles. I happened to grab a tape with a familiar Disney title from his collection. I proudly popped it in the video player while the children and adults sat anxiously around the TV to watch this new and exciting television show. Lo and behold, it was not the title! It was one of his porn flicks and they were right in the middle of a "sweating" scene!!! NO NO NO!!! I hadn't even noticed the tape was not rewound! The adults screamed while the children's heads turned upside down trying to figure it out! Parents grabbed their children one by one and ran out the door. I had only wished one had grabbed me! I was in shock and sooo embarrassed! How would I ever live that down? I didn't! They understood and laughed about it later, but my videos were no longer welcome! LOL! My pastor did jokingly say, "Now, Evangelist Wright, if you have any extra…." I slapped him on the back and told him to shut up! He knew they were not my tapes!!!

After our term in Germany, we were relocated to Ft. Campbell, Kentucky, which is approximately 60 miles from Music City, USA—Nashville, Tennessee. I worked faithfully for my church in Clarksville, Tennessee, a small community located right outside the military base. I was the music director for my local church and for my Church of God in Christ jurisdiction. We had a choir with no instrumentalists, but we sang as though we missed nothing! Acapella singing wasn't strange for me because I had plenty of training during our prayer meetings in Ft. Knox. We would find a key, build harmony, and we had church!

I became a member of a community choir called People Helping People in Clarksville. It was a choir composed of neighboring churches coming together to raise money for Christmas for less fortunate children, and my church needed a representative. Guess who! While there, I became close friends with a musician named Daryl Bowers. He asked if I would go with him to Nashville to meet a television personality named Bobby Jones who was looking for a soprano for his group.

All I saw was the opportunity for employment. I had searched and searched for a job on the military base and its surrounding areas. No employment available anywhere. Officers' wives and residents of the area had the employment market tied up. Enlisted military families often suffer from a lack of revenue, and Wayne and I were suffering. Due to the unavailability of work in the area, I commuted to and from my hometown of Indianapolis, Indiana—a four-hour drive— to find work so that we could live. Naturally, I jumped on the possibility of this opportunity becoming revenue for us.

I nervously drove to Nashville for the audition. I had sung all my life but had never had to audition. That was scary!!! I arrived at the church where Bobby Jones' workers greeted me and were ever so kind. Daryl had spoken so highly of me that Bobby was eagerly anticipating my arrival. His keyboard player for the evening was the great Mervyn Warren of the famous acapella group, Take 6. Mervyn played for me that night as I auditioned with a song by The Clark Sisters, "Is My Living in Vain," and he expressed his admiration for the talent God had given me.

Is it possible this could be work for me? Could this be the employment I needed for my family? Is this real life? Is there really such a thing as singing and getting a check for it? Well, yes, I got the call and yes, I got the job, or so I thought! Bobby "hired" me for a group called Nashville, but no money was involved, only exposure. *Exposure, who can live off exposure?* Exposure wouldn't pay the bills, but God and His infinite ways used this exposure to open the doors to the profession of singing studio sessions!

Bobby then recognized my administrative "banking" skills and asked me to be his assistant. Now I was getting somewhere! Bobby's music director, Derrick Lee, watched me intently. He heard a sound that I carried, but at the time, I didn't understand what he heard. He'd say to me, "Angie, you have something on you, girl. You have a wonderful gift. You sing, honey; you don't holler! Do not allow the lack of affirmation to determine your destination. You are somebody in Christ with a gift for which you are accountable. Don't allow all the whooping that Black Gospel music requires to ruin your voice. Angie, you have a voice that can reach black *and* white people. I see you singing for a white audience, so while you are here, you just stand flat-footed and sing, honey. Put your gospel gown on and let it flow along with your notes. Be grand, honey; just be grand!" He told Bobby "This child has got something on her, and you ought to recognize it! I see it, honey, and it's grand!" Bobby did listen and moved me from the group called Nashville, composed of about 18 people, to his more elite group known as New Life, who filmed weekly for his television show titled *Bobby Jones Gospel.*

From here, I became known as a professional background vocalist and not a Sunday School teacher! What in the world was God up to?

Bobby Jones and New Life

CHAPTER 2
BACKGROUND VOCALIST
– THE PROFESSION

Life with Bobby Jones' New Life Singers was totally life-changing for me. We worked, ate, studied, performed, and lived together. We were a family! With all families there is, and must be, order. We had ours, though silently spoken. Bobby Jones was the father; Azell Futrell was our on-the-road pastor (manager); Derrick Lee was the big brother who wasn't afraid to buck the father; and Emily Harris was our mother, who feared no one!

At 23 years of age, I was vulnerable and learning *(still learning at 58!)*. Having lost my mother at age 18, I have always sought out "mothering" and mature women's wisdom wherever I went. Emily immediately filled that role of mother for me while on the road! She mothered us all, and her love included encouragement, as well as discipline.

Emily was *sooo* clean with a refreshing smell about her and her clothes! I wondered how someone could smell so good all the time. She began to teach me, as I inquired. She said, "Honey, every woman needs to wear non-talc powder every day, especially on the stage where you'll sweat. Baby, you must take showers often. Your suitcase should be full of things to enhance your inward and outward beauty." She advised, "Honey, get up early enough in the morning to get your thoughts together; drink a cup of coffee to relax yourself, and then prepare yourself for the world."

Her toiletry bag could fill a regular size carry-on suitcase. She had sprays for everything. Her makeup case was more extensive than any makeup counter at any department store! Her underclothes had special bags. Her shoes had cases that looked like Hollywood shoe bags.

I remember one time landing in Jamaica where we were bombarded with bellhops trying to take our luggage for a tip. It seemed like hundreds of them came toward us all at once. All of them smelled like they had been exposed to the sun for a week without a bath. It was suffocating! We couldn't breathe because fresh air escaped us in the mass of these workers who were determined to be paid. Our only refuge was diving into Emily's underarm. It smelled so good. She laughed at us diving into her like she was a mother hen! It saved us! She was screaming, "Listen here!!! Listen here!!! Y'all trying to kill me!" We were fighting as to who could get the closest so we could breathe! That was the turning point for me. I made up my mind to always smell good enough for refuge!

Emily watched over us girls and our attire. She was our model for style. She always inspected what we wore on stage to minister; nothing shabby for her girls.

I overheard a conversation she was having with Francine

Belcher, the alto singer of the group. They were discussing her slip. Francine had lost weight, and her slip kept sliding down. Emily said, "Baby girl, now you need to pin that. That's too big!" Francine, not having a pin, decided to just knot it on the side and sing on. We got through a few songs safely, but *baaa-by*...we looked up around the third or fourth song and Francine was singing with her slip around her ankles! It was over for us! Bent over from laughing and trying not to make her uncomfortable or more embarrassed than she already was, we attempted discreetly to tell her to kick it over to the side of the stage and keep singing.

As discreet as we tried to be in the situation, Dr. Bobby Jones felt our hesitancy and saw us looking at Francine and followed our eyes down to the floor. He could not keep it to himself and felt the need to include the audience in our dilemma. We were in shock that he vocalized it; we laughed again! Things always happened on stage, but Derrick made sure we kept the show together!

New Life's Powerhouses
Nuana Dunlap and Beverly Crawford were God's gift to New Life. Bobby Jones traveled the world and sought talent, in the body of Christ, for his weekly television show. He would often come to his office, where I was his secretary, and we'd discuss talent that he had witnessed over the weekend during his emcee engagements. He would be so excited to share what the people had done and who he had met and was always mesmerized by power-packed talent. If you weren't inhibited, he would showcase it! Artists throughout the years have been introduced to the world by his global television show.

Bobby would gather videos of auditions for his show. He would be fascinated by the talent presented to him, both good and bad. If they were bad, he would not allow you to talk about them, but instead would simply move on to the next video. He was fair when it came to talent. He knew everyone was not called to it, but it didn't stop them from seeking their purpose. The schoolteacher in Bobby always leaked from his perspective and we respected it, even though we didn't agree all the time. After *every* show he instructed us on how to do better.

Sometimes it was okay, but other times we were just plum tired! After singing all night, working the "altar" with these girls, no one wanted to hear a word. It was our goal to get off stage and run to our bunks on the bus to dodge the hour of Bobby Jones' "teaching." After all, he was the father of the group, and we knew he had the right to say anything he wanted to say *(and most times he did!)*. After the show, while traveling to the next city, Bobby would lecture us while waiting to stop for food. If not then, you always had tomorrow morning on the bus! The look on Derrick's face when this would happen was priceless!

I must say, we did learn from the lessons taught by Dr. Jones. If he wasn't teaching verbally, he was teaching from the video tapes of his shows or from videos submitted to him from various artists who wanted to be on his show. He had a one-track mind—*Bobby Jones Gospel*. He knew what he was called and gifted to do, and that's what he did. His focus remained strictly on his television show.

Powerhouse Number One

One day when leaving Bobby's office to get on the bus for the weekend, he said, "Angela, when you get on the bus, I have a surprise for you!" I couldn't imagine what it could be! When I stepped on the bus, I saw this little, short woman sitting on the couch with her legs swinging because they couldn't reach the floor! This lady had the biggest smile ever and she wore a little white doily-style head covering. OMG! She was precious to me. I loved her at first sight!

Dr. Jones introduced Nuana Dunlap to the group, and we all welcomed her! Bobby knew I was Pentecostal, so he introduced her to me as his gift to me! *(LOL!)* She was and is to this day a gift to me! Watching Emily look at that doily on Nuana's head was *sooo* funny!!! Miss "Makeup of the Century" knew she had her work cut out for her! We got to know each other on the way to our date in New York. When this quiet and sweet little lady hit the stage, all hell broke loose! Literally, demons were mad at the power she presented during her time of ministry. I watched her as her gift split the atmosphere! She meant business and demons knew it! With my mouth wide open and eyes trying to keep up with where she was skipping, I thought, *Oh, my Lord...this woman is going to be work! I'm going to have to work harder than any revival I've ever sung for! She doesn't know when to quit and Your power in her is overwhelming even to her! Father God, she's about to explode! Help her, Jesus, help her, because I don't know what to do with this!* We were all in shock as Bobby looked on her with the pride of a father. He knew he had not disclosed to us all of who she was, and he was so tickled by our reaction, as well as that of the audience. He knew *exactly* what he had unleashed on us...and it was marvelous! Although I had sung for churches my entire life,

I had never witnessed anything like her. If Google had already been invented, I would have googled her! What in the world was she?!

Dr. Jones expressed to me that he knew she didn't wear pants or makeup, but we had to do something to enhance her facial features for television. Nuana would now become a regular on his television show and the lights from the cameras would wash her out. I was given the task of breaking this news to her. We knew Mother Emily would have been too much!

As gently and sweetly as I could, I explained to her the importance of television ministry as a means of reaching the masses; we must be seen by cameras and not washed out. I explained to her the importance of wearing makeup for the cameras. In turn, she admitted that makeup was not something she desired to wear and had never worn it. She didn't like the boldness of it and all the colors. She expressed to me that she never wanted to be a distraction from God's ministry. I could not have agreed with her more, but we had to do what was required to be effective in this new avenue of ministry—television.

We agreed to disagree. She just was not feeling makeup at all! I asked her if we could meet halfway and assured her that we were not trying to make her look clownish. I told her that she could even pick out her own makeup. She insisted on looking natural, so I told her that I would apply it so lightly that she would never know it was there.

Nuana went to the store to purchase her makeup for the taping that evening and returned with all-natural makeup. When I say natural, I mean *clear* everything! She was *sooo* happy with it being uncolored and I sat there frustrated because it enhanced nothing! I reported to Bobby that this was his "baby" and it was going to take time to break this "horse" in. She was not going to be an "overnight" success! This is where Emily would wave her towel in the air and say, "I'm not fooling with that!" We had to win her trust over time to get makeup on her for the cameras and that doily off her head! Let it be known that it was only for TV; once Nuana returned home to Flint, Michigan to her father's church, she wouldn't miss a beat in respecting her denomination. She never changed her beliefs; doily on…makeup off! We loved her for her strong convictions and God honored her for it. Whatever it takes for that person to feel closer to God, let it be. As long as it doesn't speak against His holiness, God is pleased. This was powerhouse number one!

Powerhouse Number Two

Tons of audition videos constantly arrived by mail for Bobby to consider for his show. As we watched these submitted videos in the back of the bus, one particular video stood out. It was a video of a group of sisters singing from Gainesville, Florida. Dr. Jones loved their charisma and stage presence. He invited them to the show and fell in love with one singer in particular in the group. Her name was Beverly Crawford, Evangelist Beverly Crawford, that is! She never demanded a title, but in witnessing her ministry, one would never have a problem giving it to her!

Both Nuana and Beverly were raised by strong, pastoral fathers who taught them to minister at all times, whatever the cost. They were taught to go for the jugular vein of the enemy, and they did! They were taught to give each ministry opportunity everything they had. Every time they ministered it was as if it was their last chance to do so. You could never anticipate what the Lord was going to do through them. They were quiet and prayerful backstage but became God's trumpet on stage. *Boyyyeee*, when Bobby would release them to do what they did, you knew to hold on with all your might because you were going for a ride! I have always loved rollercoasters, and these two were always my thrill in the ministry. You would know they had prepared to hear from God, and they were always obedient to perform His works. It was simply amazing being a background vocalist to such a calling as theirs. Nuana's father is a bishop and Beverly's father was a pastor. They were taught to be all things to all men every time. Growing up, they had witnessed the prayer times and the altar prayer lines of their parents and they carried their mantles everywhere they went.

Nuana was a little more reluctant to be out front, but something would happen when she heard the music and it was her time to sing. God would always take charge and swing her around into a "superwoman" episode. You knew it was not her doing a thing, but God. She would have a look of abandonment about her and you knew change had taken place! After the show, we would be so amused by her quiet persona, knowing what damage she had just done to the kingdom of satan. We would pick on her and she would just smile and "plead the fifth" to say it wasn't her!

Now Evangelist Beverly was from another spectrum. She was not bashful at all backstage or on stage. She knew what she had come to do, and her teaching as a woman minister was not to be inhibited. She came with a sickle in her hand, and as a woman, she was not afraid to use it! Preach, teach, lay hands, cast out, hold-up or kick-down—she was trained to do it, and she did.

Beverly had a way of telling a story in her song that would catch you up in the glory of it all by the end of the song, which always resulted in a victory shout and dance. You would dance whether the song was fast or slow. The victory presented in it was always a cause for celebration. Beverly's emotion depicted in her singing was so contagious that one would dance because her dog got a new bone! Her dance was so infectious that you never wanted to waste an opportunity to rejoice with her. It would start off as a slow song with her, but never ended as one. She would always present a reason to dance and praise the Lord!

One had to watch carefully to see Beverly and Nuana's camaraderie on stage. They tag-teamed all the time. One would somehow know to start and allow the other to finish. They both knew that we, as background vocalists, were equipped to follow their leading wherever the Lord led. We could even tell by their shoulder movement what they were about to do next. As background vocalists, we knew how to manage the called mission every time. I knew that if a high note was reached, I had the responsibility to reinforce it with my gifting while they went on to another note. When the call and answer activity in a song began, one would call and we would answer every time, and sometimes even with a unified step!

The band was phenomenal! They never tried to control the moving of the Spirit as musicians often do. These band members flowed with us as we were led by the Lord. Most times, vamps were created on the spot. We knew never to place God in a box of a song. When a phrase was repeated, that was our cue to repeat and drive it home. The power of God was mesmerizing. Healings and deliverances took place when we, as a people, were on one accord. The band would catch the phrase God was using at that moment and Derrick would stomp it out on the keys and his musicians followed. We would hear them, and they were listening to us, and we would rejoice in the new sound God had just given us! The girls would sing with all their might, the band would play with all their power, and the audience would join in with praise and dance. Sometimes a vamp would last for hours, and we never tired. Whether it was laying on of hands, rebuking sickness and disease, praying with them, hugging them, crying with them, or simply laying on the floor with them, we worked with God's people until He was through. We were all altar workers from our churches and knew how to work until breakthrough came. The joy of The Lord would take over and we would be in the moment of what God was doing for His people. We knew never to allow an effort to go dormant, so we always rendered our ability to the cause of a successful time of ministry on stage. The Lord always revealed to us what He was doing, and we followed.

With protocol in place, everyone knew their position and was respected. However, when God took over, everyone knew to allow Him to have His way. It was always amazing!!!

An Unspoken Protocol
There was an unspoken protocol within the New Life group among the female singers. We had our two powerhouses, and whatever they were led to do on stage, Emily, Francine, and I were ready and covered them. We knew to pray and sing at the same time. We wanted God's will to be done every time we hit the stage. We trusted the leading of the Lord and followed them as they followed Christ. We knew when a vamp was sung to pace ourselves because these girls could sing for hours. They would work an altar call or prayer line at the end of any song, and we had to be ready. We were always ready!

They would grace the front of the stage to encourage, lay hands, and grab someone to shout with them. At any given moment they could be pulled off the stage. We were always covering and ready to snatch them back to safety! They would simply lose themselves in the Holy Ghost while having full confidence that we had their backs. Sometimes all we could catch was the hem of their garment to keep them from toppling over off the stage. They would operate in the Spirit and we were left to "clean up aisle three." (LOL!)

When I first started in the group, I was the dancer and would just shout. Well…our big brother, Derrick, pulled me to the side to correct me. With a stern, yet loving, voice, he informed me that rejoicing, getting happy and dancing is only the benefit of what we do. He said, "Angela, you are hired to SING, not shout. I have only one soprano and when you dismiss yourself to shout, I have lost the sound of the group. Either you learn to sing while you are shouting, or there will be no shouting. Singing is what we are expecting and what you shall do. Okay suga' plum?" After he made that clear, as only a big brother could, I learned to shout and sing at the same time! *Ohhh*, the power of the Lord worked mightily through our team and we loved being used by Him!

Bahamas Gospel Explosion

Bobby Jones took his Gospel Explosion experience to the Bahamas. New Life had some time off, so we prepared to enjoy the beach. I had purchased some rhinestone sandals that I thought would be cute on the beach. While on shore, we decided to wade in the water. Not wanting my expensive sandals to get wet, I left them safely up shore. Then to my surprise, a wave came and washed away one of my $50 sandals! I saw my shoe riding that wave and was devastated, yet determined, to retrieve it!

Jumping in and almost drowning, I rescued my shoe and swung it in the air while screaming, "I got my shoe! I got my shoe!" Nuana started hollering and running towards me frantically and screaming, "Get down, Angie!!! Drop down in the water! Angie, drop down!" Not understanding what she was saying and knowing it couldn't be more important than me having my shoe, I wondered what could possibly be the problem. I was smiling and thinking I had won; I got the prize—my shoe. To my astonishment, the shoe was not my only prize. The tide had swept over me and had given me a swimsuit filled completely with sand. The sand left no room for my body! The weight of the sand had pulled the swimsuit away from my body and, thus, resulted in it hanging on my side like a bad diaper. I stood there with my shoe in hand, naked as a jaybird!

When I finally followed Nuana's eyes and looked down to see what she was looking at and screaming about, I discovered my dilemma, and before I could take cover, she dived on me like a blanket! We both succumbed to the water while she was digging out the sand from my swimsuit and shouting, "Don't get up! Don't get up!" This had to be the most embarrassing moment of my life, but I did have my shoe! LOL! Needless to say, there was no more walking on the beach for me, and to this day, I don't do beaches…and I still have my shoe!

Left Behind

My travels with New Life continued to expand. We accepted an invitation to minister on the beautiful island of Bermuda. Although I consented to go, I must admit the legend of the Bermuda Triangle did concern me. In order to travel to

this foreign island, we needed passports or official birth certificates. We were told that copies of our birth certificates would
suffice. All flights leaving from New York to Bermuda were
very early, so we had to travel the day before in order to catch
that early morning flight.

We arrived in New York and went straight to the hotel
for our night's stay. When we arrived at the hotel, you could
hear a pin drop. It was a dump! The hotel was atrocious! We
were scared to death. Bobby consoled the group with the fact
that it was only one night. Entering the rooms, we saw the
bedspreads were nasty, and our beds were sitting on bricks.
The toilets weren't clean, nor flushed, and the room had roach-
es! We were told we were being squeamish. Nuana and I decided we were not staying in those rooms overnight. It was
just one night, so we decided to stay up. But where? All night I
crocheted and Nuana prayed while sitting in the hotel's bar! By
morning, we were spent! No worries, though; we were on our
way to a resort where we would rest comfortably.

We arrived at the airport to board and at the gate, the
airline's agent rejected our copied birth certificates. *What?!
What do you mean copies are not acceptable?!* Those who had
originals were able to board the plane. They said I had a fit! All
I could see was being left in New York in that lowdown hotel!
I do remember breaking down and crying because my family
had to leave us behind. There were four of us without proper
paperwork, but my "road pastor," Azell, my "father," Bobby,
and my "mother," Emily, were boarding without us. We had
to have our birth certificates overnighted to the airport and
then fly out in the morning. Bobby gave us a credit card to use
to get a cab and go to a nicer room for the evening. I was just
devastated! Azell said as he boarded the plane, he heard me
crying and screaming, "Azell, please! Please, don't leave me!

Azell, please don't leave me here!!!" He said I sounded like a wife being left by her husband!

I remember getting to the hotel, but I don't even remember sleeping. I was so tired and distraught, I passed out. They said we slept like babies. Nuana said she checked on me to see if I was still breathing. The next day the certificates arrived, and we did make it safely to join the others *(with much attitude, may I add? LOL!)*.

Floating Airplanes

To get to one of our island engagements we once had to ride floating aircrafts, which are airplanes that land in the water and float to shore when runways are not available on land. We noticed the pilot looking frantic as we approached him from around the corner to board the plane. With his hand extended, he motioned for us to stop. He reached for his huge cell phone and dialed someone and began to speak very aggressively, in a fussing manner. We didn't know what was going on.

Azell approached him to ask if there was a problem. He returned after their conversation to tell us the man had to order an additional plane. He said we were too heavy for one plane! He told Azell when he saw us coming around the corner to get on his plane, he knew he needed help to get us across the water. Sure enough, another plane was ordered, and they strategically set us on each plane by weight! He told us later that one plane would not have survived the water landing. He said we would have sunk! *Whatever!*

Custom Tour Buses

I so enjoy sleeping on custom tour buses. The motion of the bus rocks me to sleep while the bunk cuddles me. However, they are not free of troubles. Custom buses are expensive to purchase and rent. If the artist you are traveling with owns the bus, they are expensive to repair. If the artist is renting the bus, sometimes they are not modern or renovated. I have had to travel in both scenarios, with the owner and the renter. Either way, it requires prayers, patience, and understanding. Prayers that it makes it, patience if you're delayed, and understanding if you don't make it.

Emily hated the buses with the velvet interior. She would say, "Lord, I'm sleeping in a coffin tonight!" We would all holler with laughter! It was not unusual for us to have to stop at a store to get cleaning supplies for the bus to enable us to just breathe! Sometimes the smell of diesel was *sooo* overwhelming due to improper ventilation. Conditions were sometimes so bad on a bus that all we could do was laugh about it and pray to get to our destination quickly. We learned to cope by getting on the bus and going to sleep. Sleep would be our escape! Nyquil and Alka Seltzers would remedy the cough we would have and expedite sleep.

I went to have a physical one year, and the doctor came and sat beside me with a solemn look on her face that frightened me. I asked her what she had found. She told me that she understood I was a minister, but I had to quit drinking alcohol because I was causing irreparable damage to my liver. She said my enzyme levels were off the chart. I expressed to her that I did not drink. She consoled me and advised me to be honest with her and to quit the drinking. At this time, I began to cry because I wasn't convincing her that I was not a drunk. I didn't even drink wine! My doctor calmed me down and asked if I was taking any medications and I told her no. She asked if I was taking any over-the-counter drugs and, again, I told her no, nothing except Nyquil. She shouted, "That's it! You are consuming too much of it and it's killing you!" Needless to say, I laid off the bottle—the Nyquil bottle, that is.

Once, we were on a bus that was having trouble and could not exceed beyond 20 mph. One of the singers sat in the window and began to wave at the people like we were on a float in a parade! We hollered laughing because the people returned her wave with a look that said, "Who is on that slow, parade-moving, must-be-important bus!"Ralph Lofton was our wonderful organist as well as our entertainment. He was hilarious! He had the uncanny ability to hear a song being played and sing along with it in a totally different key. It would rub our ears so wrong and he would not stop! You would have to stop what you were doing to hear what you thought you heard. It would mess with your head because it was amazingly wrong! I would try to encourage him to get on the right key by saying, "Lift it, LIFT it; you're almost there!" Instead of lifting the note, he would stretch his neck and continue to repeat the same wrong note. His neck would eventually stretch to twice its normal length while he sang the song in yet another key. That would tickle us sooo bad because it was wrong, and he looked crazy!

Recapping the shows on the bus were fun times, too. We could express what worked and what didn't. This was the time to acknowledge the works of God throughout the evening and share testimonies of His works through us. Some shows were harder than others, as some people were receptive, and others were skeptical. But as a team, we worked with them all. What God did through New Life was nothing less than miraculous. The testimonies of God at work through us were overwhelming. God did get the Glory! To this day, the testimonies still come!

We loved each other dearly. When one laughed, we all laughed. When one cried, we all cried. We were definitely a team divinely orchestrated by God, and to this day, we still love each other. Even though ministry has led us down different paths, the love between us will never change.

Leap of Faith – Relocation

Meanwhile, back at the ranch—or should I say, my ranch—my husband became more and more frequent in adulterous affairs. I would forgive him and the women and, through love, lead them to the Lord *(The Ministry of Forgiveness—that's another book!)*. It was as if my forgiveness only cleaned his pallet for the next affair. Old school church mothers would say "pray 'em through." I prayed and he never got through! When he became engaged to another woman while we were yet married, I knew then that things were pretty serious, and I was quickly becoming the third wheel. His mistress explained to me that she was pregnant with his child. They told me they were in love and planned to marry, so I knew I had to make a decision for my life.

I prayed to God for a way out. I knew this could not be His purpose for my life. I was afraid of disease, which I had already experienced with him, and the feeling of abandonment that always follows the actions of adultery. I spent my days looking under "lampshades" trying to figure out what my husband was doing and to be prepared for decisions that did not include me. This was not living.

I knew with the decision he was about to make, I had either to return to Indianapolis to my family or take a leap of faith and move to Nashville permanently. If Nashville was my choice, I needed to work. I needed a career and wondered if a singing career was trustworthy. God knew the plans He had for me! *(Lord Jesus, I feel a shout coming on!)* My rejection by my husband became my transportation to a new life. Divorced, alone, in a strange city, and with a job of "exposure," I wholeheartedly pursued God.

New Home

Now watch this. Azell told me he had a place where I could stay in Nashville to continue my work as a singer if that's what I desired to do. With this offer, I left everything I knew, including my adulterous husband, who I believed *did* love me, but just didn't know *how.* I couldn't spend the rest of my life on hold, wondering if I was his wife or the next contestant. It was time to trust God with the life He'd given me on earth and move forward seeking His plan for me. He was working all the while.

Not understanding why I could not hold the attention of my husband, who was the love of my life, I began to seek it from other men. During the stress of this transition, I lost a ton of weight. The men winked at me and I winked back. The desire for a man led me down a backslidden path. I was singing saved songs but not living a saved life. *But God loved me better than I loved myself.* He had His hand on me! He loved me even though I turned my back on Him for the lust of my flesh.

Nuana was a prayer warrior who prayed for me end-lessly. I would hear her in the middle of the night going before God on my behalf. OMG! She didn't call out my name. No, she screamed my name! I would get so scared because I *knew* I knew better. Nuana was rebuking sins that I was now dabbling in. She was "reading my mail"! I would only go so far, but any distance with the devil is too far. I was playing right in the devil's playpen. I used my "exposure" to draw all men unto me! I needed to be rescued from myself. I needed grace and He gave it!

My New Singing Husband

God sent a man out of Columbus, Ohio, named John Primm, to rescue me from myself. He put a stop to all my inquiries.

John Primm

John and Angie

I met John in Nashville, in 1990, at a Bobby Jones Gospel Explosion. He came as a registrant to sing on the show that evening. After signing in, he asked me if I was married and I replied no. From that point on, he watched me like a hawk as I performed my duties as administrator of the event. I was complimented, but also made nervous by his tenacity. He would not stop staring or move away from the area. *(Who, except a stalker, does that?)* I would look up and he would be leaning against the wall smiling ever-so-slightly in a way that said I was beautiful to him. I was blushing all night. MiMi was there. She said, "Angie, do you see this man looking at you? Girl, don't you flirt with that grown man. He looks serious."

Needless to say, I was enjoying the attention. He had no idea I was a singer. When I finished performing that night, he latched onto me and would not leave my side. I told him I had a boyfriend and he was in the building somewhere. He stated, "Yes, he is a boy and just a friend. If he was serious, he wouldn't allow me to be this close to you. I know I won't allow him to get this close to you ever again."

That night, John told me that God told him I was his wife and asked if we could go and have coffee after the show. *(Hold On!!! Wait A Minute!)* MiMi was there with me and she was screaming, "Angie, he's moving in on you too fast!!! No, girl, don't you do it! Respect yourself!" I did respect myself and set it up where he would pursue me if he was serious. I told him I don't go to drink coffee with strangers at 11:00 at night. He told me he was returning to Columbus that night, but when his feet hit the Tennessee border again, it would be to pursue me. We exchanged phone numbers and our monthly telephone bills were astronomical. Sometimes my telephone bill was $900, enough to pay a house mortgage!

John was in pursuit and we married one year later, and that was 29 years ago. Glory to God! God was putting the pieces together in my life, applying grace, His unmerited favor. He can do anything but fail! Without your permission, His plans for you have a way of sneaking up on you.

CHAPTER 3
BACKGROUND VOCALIST
IN THE STUDIO

I was a soprano for Dr. Bobby Jones for years. We were hired as supporting vocalists for Dolly Parton, Barbara Mandrell, Wayne Newton, Aretha Franklin and various other television personalities and events.

Bobby introduced me to studio work, also known as "sessions." A session is when someone is making a record or has written a song and needs a singer to sing it for them. I was always hired to sing soprano or alto. You would go into a studio and harmonize with other singers to make the sound of the song, which are the "background vocals." You are paid per hour or per song.

People would see me on television and call into Bobby's office asking to hire me for their session work. He'd book me on sessions around Nashville. Sessions added significant revenue to my income, along with the weekend work with New Life. In 1986, this began my professional background vocalist career, otherwise known as "BGVing."

With God's continued favor, I began to get work. I never compromised the Gospel of Jesus or His holiness to obtain work. God shielded and I guarded my reputation in the work I contracted and performed. Some singers would sell out by misrepresenting Christ for a $50.00 session. They would sing, dress, perform, and do other unmentionable duties for any amount, desperate to be seen and heard.

I valued my reputation as a godly woman more than I did the mighty dollar. His holiness will shine through you when you love Him. God will provide and prepare a table before you in the presence of your enemies. I was able to say, "No, thank you; that's not a session that is lyrically correct for Christianity. I won't be able to help you" in the face of desperation, needing the money, but not willing to carry a tainted reputation.

Respect is everything. If you don't have it for yourself, don't expect others to have it for you. Be careful of your hunger. It will make you sell your birthright. Be careful of your cravings which can lead you astray.

If you're hungry, satan can certainly make his stones look like delicious bread. If it's gold you want, he knows how to make it shine. If it's fame you desire, he knows how to connect you to the serpent who beguiles you with the world's affirmations. *(Now hold that thought.)*

Hard-Working Soprano
I learned and loved to stay in the background to assure that everyone had a firm foundation on which to work. At this point as a professional, I desired to be known as the

hardest working soprano around. I never wanted anyone to feel cheated by paying me. I labored to do my best even when circumstances were not ideal.

Once I became known as a *Bobby Jones Gospel* singer, the studio work came pouring in from everywhere. While others were aspiring to be the singer with a record deal, I just wanted to work. *I love working!* People embraced the presence of Jesus I had been able to carry and hired me for work. God's favor is always at work in my life; He continues to open and close doors. He is at work all the time.

The Art of Vocal Blending

There is a difference between a background vocalist and a lead singer. Most times, a lead singer has such a profound sound that it cannot blend with other singers to create a track of harmony for a recording. There is an art to background singing, and not everyone is called to do it. You must learn to disappear and become one with other singers in order to create a chord with voices that enhances the song you are hired to sing. You must have an ear to hear the various parts in a music track which are played for you to sing.

God paired me up with a wonderful singer who has become my sister. Her name is Gale Mayes. She has the most "blendable," velvety voice in the world. She never demands to be heard, just hired. People love her for her talent, as well as her attitude. She is always pleasant and unassuming. Since Gale is so easy to work with, people love having her in the studio amidst hard work. It's easier to get things done when people are sweet and teachable.

Arrogance is your enemy behind any mic. You are hired for a session to be creative, not to cause problems that cost the producers more money. The longer you're in the studio, the more it runs against the budget to get things done. Suggestions are just what they are: *suggestions*, and *not* demands. When you continue to debate about "your suggestions" and insist on singing them, you complicate matters and prolong the session.

Bottom line, you are called to sing *their* song, not yours. Give them what they want, get your check, and go home. That know-it-all chip on your shoulder will cost you work because people will not want to hire you. You are to enter a studio with a kind spirit and willingness to work. This is what gets you hired.

Gale and I have worked sessions together for more than thirty years now and it has been wonderful! I'm blessed to be able to call her sister!

Union and Non-Union Sessions

There are session singers in Nashville who earn six digit incomes. Master sessions pay big. You are paid per pass, meaning you are paid a fee for every time you sing a particular part in a song. For example, if I sang the song "Mary Had A Little Lamb" one time, I'm paid over $200.00 for that pass. If they want a thicker sound and I double myself (stack it), then I'm paid an additional fee because that's considered another pass of that song. You normally sing three passes per song.

Let it be known, producers are not wanting to pay this type of money; it's a negotiated fee from the union. One famous producer told us that once we join the union and charge union fees, we should not expect to get a call from him for work again.

Most clients can't afford to pay this rate; only record labels have this type of budget. As the old folks say, "Baby, choose your battles!" You could be an exclusive union singer and work with union affiliates only, or you can work when you're called. The latter has been how I have survived. However, there are those who are strictly unionized singers and they do quite well! Unfortunately for me, union singers had their clique and I could not afford to wait on an annual call for a union session. If it's a good year, I might get two union calls within the year. *(Ain't nobody got time for that!)*

Follow the Leader and Learn

I have been blessed to be mentored by a master session leader. Raymond "Chip" Davis has called me for work throughout the years and has blessed my career with mounds of work in the studio. He is famous for doing sessions alone and can change his voice from strong wind to light air in a second!

He navigates a session like none other. Gale and I simply get on each side of him, behind one mic, hold on to his arms, and literally creatively flow! We can tell by his body language which direction he is going and how to follow him. Each of us can hear something in the music track that no one else hears, and we dare to sing it! If you put an idea out there, be ready to follow through because the artist may want to change the entire measure, or measures, of the song to implement your idea.

You're saying, "Yes! That's what I heard!" while the other singers are looking at you and thinking, "I wish you'd heard that four passes ago! Now we have to start over to implement your idea! Gee, thanks!" And how do you know that's what they're thinking? It's all in a look without anyone having to say a word! LOL! You would be saying the same thing if it were them coming up with new ideas and the song is about over. Then you have to backtrack and create around the new idea. Sometimes this process is fun! Other times it's, "*Hush!* Quit creating and let's go home!" We have a way of telling each other to shut up without the producer reading our signals.

Chip can walk you through the hardest arrangements with ease. What you can't hear, he can. He then becomes your "training wheels" to the particular part you're missing. He will sing it in your ear until the chord registers in your mind. It's sometimes challenging to hear vocal parts with extensive instrumentation, but he's saying, "Listen, baby; you are right here. Listen to me." When we just can't get it, he says "Here, sing my part and I'll sing yours." Then, he sings straight into the stratosphere as high as any soprano and will come back down to the tenor part to finish his pass.

He makes me so mad sometimes, singing too high! He tells me, "Angie, it's higher. I need you to go higher! It's a high inversion." I'm screaming back, "No! Are you crazy?! Nobody sings that high! God says, "Low, I am with you!" It's amazing to witness, but eventually he will fuss me into the part. I'm pouting but singing to get it done. He won't quit until he hears what he wants.

Chip loves what he does, just don't mention "religion" to him. He will sit and give you a three-hour sermon on what he doesn't like about a thirty-minute sermon! He's our brother, though, and we love him dearly. He has supported, taught, encouraged and loved Gale and me for years. I'm so grateful for his believing in us and molding us for the aggressive sound of Nashville music.

Creating Accompaniment Tracks

Tyrone Dickerson is another producing brother of mine. He is contracted by a record label that purchases licenses of popular Black Gospel songs to produce accompaniment tracks.

There are churches who cannot find or afford live musicians for their services and will use these tracks for the music ministry of their church. You will find this more and more in young and upcoming churches. Tracks are no longer strange to the ministry.

I have found tracks to be lifesaving for me. Trying to hire musicians with their various schedules is oftentimes difficult. My motto is: "Have tracks will travel!" Please note that there is nothing that can replace live music. The flexibility, camaraderie and the flow of a live band cannot ever be replaced with the inflexibility of an accompaniment track.

Tyrone hires musicians to play the songs to be recorded for the day. We call this "laying the track." Then, on the following day, the singers come to record the background vocals for the song. Finally, after a mixing process, the accompaniment tracks are made available for leasing purposes to artists for custom projects or churches in need of music. For each song, he cleverly provides a high and low version for male or female singers.

Singing All Parts

I was hired to do a ten-song session alone, meaning I sang all the parts. I got to the end of the session, and they wanted bass singing on one of the songs. My question was, "How much does it pay?" I did it and was paid! This is the life of a singer, so don't judge me!

I have a god-sister who works for a Christian television network. They advertised on their network the ability to record your custom project at their famous facility. People contacted her office after seeing the advertisement and scheduled a time to come and record their music. Upon scheduling their recordings, she recommended the studio's musicians and singers, which was oftentimes me. If they had no preferences, we'd get the jobs to record their project/record.

It was a wonderful account to have! Sometimes these sessions consisted of 14 songs, and I would be the only singer to do all parts and stacks. We'd get it done by the end of the day because there were no other singers with different ideas. But by the end of that day, I didn't even want to hear myself talk!

People would come from all over the world to record in this studio. One lady loved us so much for what we did with her music that for the next five years she sent us money ranging from $300.00 - $500.00 as a Christmas gift! I was sad when the studio was sold, but we still have a wonderful relationship.

Always Get Clarity

There was one session I was called to do for a civil rights leader and the songs were wonderful and uplifting.

He paid very well and was very pleasant. At the end of the day, I was happy. Mission accomplished!

A month later, I received a copy of the completed project in the mail and he had titled it, "I Have Kissed My Last A_ _." *(WHAT?!)* This was not my understanding and none of the lyrics were abrasive or obscene. I had been misled and was concerned about my reputation. I tried calling him and he never accepted, nor returned, my calls. I waited and wanted to let him know that this was unacceptable. However, it was done, and it was his music. He had a right to call it what he wanted, but I just believed him to respect me better. He had tricked me!!! I prayed that thing down in the heavenlies and God fixed it. It was never released mainstream! God knew my heart.

I did a session for a producer from another country who did not quite understand the logistics of an American session. He was a writer who wanted to experiment with my vocal ability. This is permissible, but time is money. The longer you're in the studio, the more one has to pay for your time. If these stipulations are not put into place, a writer can write all day and expect you to stand at the mic and sing while he writes!

I had been hired for one song which normally takes no more than one hour. As I finished the song per his instruction, he asked if I could sing it in another style. Of course, I could; however, my time is money. You can keep me all day with one song, but the meter is running. It's only fair. You can be as creative as you want, but upon hiring someone, you should be concise in your instructions and ready to get it done.

If someone hires you per hour, then rest in the fact that they are paying you to "change their minds" and try different things. You don't have to fret because you're on the clock and will be paid for the endurance of their creativity. Now, if they have explained to you upfront that they have no budget, and this one-hour session has turned to three hours and you've sung the song in more than one style, then this is a problem.

You have to stick to your rate as being a set fee per hour or per song, whichever is greater. This is a standard policy in session life. People will try to take advantage of your time and gifting. It's not that you have an attitude of entitlement; it's a business for you. This is how you survive.

You're hired to get it done. No matter how many variations they desire to hear it sung, it costs time and money—your time and their money. This is how it works, and everyone is pleased. It's called *employment!*

There is also something called a "spec" session. This is where you record a song and are not paid until the song is picked up by an artist. If you consent to this type of agreement, you could be hired and never paid.

The life of a background vocalist has been an experience. I prefer to relate to my bad experiences as learning ones, but even in remaining positive you must understand that not everyone is appreciative of your gift and will use it to benefit themselves while having no budget to pay you for your time. Payment information is something you should negotiate before you step behind a mic. Some people have good intentions but no budget. For the benefit of maintaining a healthy work relationship, it is wise to get your ducks in a row before you start so no one's feelings are hurt or misunderstood. It's just business and you must treat it as such.

Know Your Producer or Session Leader

We've had sessions where the producer told us to "run and cash the check!" He had written two checks from the same money and stated, "Whoever gets to the bank first, gets the prize!"

It's important to have a go-to person that you know will be responsible for your employment. It is not uncommon for producers to hire you on a 30-day term and forget you worked. You are left looking for a check that doesn't even exist.

The Vampire

Gale and I were called for a session where the studio was darkened and the atmosphere was eerily solemn. Knowing the producer from time past, he was more cheerful than usual in an attempt to buffer the strangeness. He stood in the door to welcome us and warned us that today's client was a "little different." Well, we never meet strangers, so we started asking, "Where is he?" He told us that the warning was necessary because the client believed he was a vampire. *WHAT?! Listen, Linda, listen!* We are black folks and we don't do scary, not even a little bit!

Upon his introduction, he seemed to stand and glide toward us to shake our hands, from which we withdrew. We were tickled and scared at the same time! Gale grabbed her necklace and looked at me and said, "Girlfriend, I got my cross around my neck and I sho' hope you ate garlic!" He was an artist on a grant from his country to sing nursery rhymes!

They were sweet songs. One song he said was slow and had a lot of "Ooos." He asked if we needed to change the ambiance by turning down the lights. Simultaneously, Gale and I said, "No! We're good!" We told him to leave those lights right where they were—ON!

Slave Sounds

During another one of our interesting session experiences, the producer, being excited and pleased with our sound, asked if we would give him a separate track of slave sounds. *(Can you say "awkward"?)* He meant to say ad-lib, but it didn't come out like that! Knowing my sister Gale, I knew that wouldn't sit well with her at all. Chip and I were a bit nervous and didn't know what to think, but Gale had an answer for him. She told him, "Give me a chain and a whip and I'll give you some slave sounds." That broke the ice, and he was so apologetic. Needless to say, the rest of the session was a little quiet. We were embarrassed for him.

Singing "On The Clock"

Gale and I had a session to sing the same two words for hours. We never complained because the session paid by the hour. It was grueling, but it paid! The client was a famous artist with money who wanted to hear these two words sung over and over again in different variations. His money and our time, job done!

If someone schedules a time slot such as a 10:00 a.m. until 2:00 p.m., this means that they are paying you by the hour and all you have to do is be ready to sing whatever it is they are requesting. Don't fret over time spent when you are on the clock. It's their dime and your time. Hush and just get paid!

Work to Please Your Client

Some session leaders can be overbearing and forget that they work for the client. During one session, while Gale and I tried to please the artist, the session leader insisted on it being his way and was not open for suggestions, not even from the artist. The artist had heard the song sung a particular way and wanted that sound for her recording. Mind you, he was not the one writing the checks! He argued while we suggested. He kept arguing, "Believe me; that is not what you want! This is what you want. I know what I'm talking about." The artist's response was that she wanted the original sound of the song. So, we stood there not getting anything done.

I and my big mouth decided to bring clarity to the situation and suggested that we stop and listen to the desires of the artist and lay down what she wanted. That was the straw that broke the camel's back. Upon this suggestion, the leader snapped his fingers and swung his arms and stomped out of the studio stating, "I will not be told what to do by mere background vocalists! Get another session leader because I am not the one!" He left us there with our mouths hung wide open. Gale and I were left wondering what had just happened.

As a background vocalist, you must understand that the client who has hired you is spending their money for the studio, engineer, and other singers. Your indecisiveness, tardiness, lack of interest, complaints, argumentativeness, grandiosity, and a desire not to cooperate costs them money. The things listed above are elements for a bad session. This is unfair to the client who hired you expecting to get the job done. You must enter a session with the mindset of being a blessing. Give your client what they want; it's due them. It should never be about you; it's about them! Your political views, your religion, and your inflexibility are not in the budget. They need to get a job done with limited time. You want to get in there and get out and save them time and money. A singer who is pleasant, listens, gives suggestions, takes instructions, gets the job done and gets out is the reputation you want to have and the only one that will keep you working. Always take their music to another level with your gift. That is why you are hired!

Gale and I showed up at one session and sang the first few songs and then the producer decided that our voices were too "heavy" of a sound for him. Now mind you, we had sung for this particular artist for years. Her trademark sound consisted of Gale and I being her background vocalists.

At this point, we were confused as to what the producer was trying to accomplish. He fired us on the spot and decided he wanted "lighter singing" singers. This resulted in the artist firing him after she heard what was done and called us back to stack over the finished project for a "heavier" sound.

One elderly, black singer, who graces all-white audiences, hired us to do her record. When we thanked her for the work, she stated, "Oh my goodness, I wouldn't think of doing a record without you people!" Ding-ding-ding; that sat wrong! LOL! Gale and I looked at each other and Gale asked me, "Does she not know she's black along with us people?" I hollered laughing! The rest of the day, Gale made faces that were priceless. Gale will do the craziest things in the studio and leave you holding the bag because she won't crack a smile. She's not right at all! I can't contain myself when I'm with her. She makes life so much fun!

Sing Through Difficulties

On one extremely hot summer day, a studio's air conditioner went out on us during the session. The singers were burning up and had to take frequent breaks to step out of the building just to breathe.

One of the session singers decided he couldn't take it anymore and decided to strip down to his underwear at the mic. Y'all! He was standing there at the mic in his drawers! I looked over and saw him and was shocked! Not only was he naked, but he was singing on a record for a United Pentecostal Church (UPC) singer who was still wearing her head covering in the control room! Needless to say, we did *not* agree with his signs of discomfort. I told him to either put his clothes back on or I was going home! I was not being paid to observe his intimates! Begrudgingly, he did redress. Lord, have mercy!

Home studios are common in Nashville. One house session we did in a bedroom. The producer used an upright mattress to absorb the room sound. That wouldn't have been so bad, but the mattress had urine stains! We sang right on, being careful not to touch the mattress. Dodging the mattress while singing caused us to laugh even more the entire time! Oh, the things we have done for the sake of singing for a living!

Gale and I showed up to do a session one evening in a factory studio with a producer she knew. He was sooo kind. We had fun singing together. We sang for about eight hours in the new studio format called "Pro Tools." Pro Tools was the craze in recording that eliminated the long process of reel-to-reel (tape) recording. Gale and I knew from experience that it had to be "saved" on the computer from time to time to keep the work. We kept advising the singer/engineer to save the work and he insisted he was fine and that he had it covered. "Just sing!" he said. We did! During the last song, at around 11:00 p.m., a thunderstorm arose. Lights went out and came back on shortly afterwards.

After the uploading of the program, he discovered that he had not saved one thing we recorded! Every background vocal we had sung was lost!!! Eight hours of work down the drain! Dumbfounded, he looked at us apologetically and we returned his look. We were sorry but we had done what we were being paid to do and suggested the saving of the work. We had to be paid the eight hours of work and to replace what was lost would be another session, another day. It could be the next day, as we were available; however, it would cost him another session. Needless to say, we did work it out. I believe from that point on he saved as he went along.

CHAPTER 4
BACKGROUND VOCALIST
IN THE COMMUNITY

Singers, God has given you a gift to sing and you do not own it. You are only responsible for it. In prayer, the Lord spoke to me and said, "I hate talent. It's the one thing that causes men to forget Me. Once they discover it, they no longer have a need for Me. I'm not impressed with their talent, for I gave it to them; I'm impressed with how they use it."

You must share your gift at every opportunity. Give your gift, and the Lord will bless you for being responsible and obedient.

Singing at Church

While everyone is being paid for everything, don't miss your blessing in giving. It's wonderful to have income, and if a paid position is available to you, even at your church, this is wonderful. Work this position with honor! But what if a paid staff member needs you to help accomplish a mission in song without pay; would you be big enough to humble yourself and say, "Sure!"; or would you say, "Uhhh, ask your paid staff, because you're not paying me"? It is right to be respected, but it is wrong to demand your position. Demanding is not humility. Never lose focus of your mission, which is the purpose of your gift. Grandness and selfishness are not of Father God. He is a giver! The attitude of grandness comes from its father, Lucifer. He demanded His place in the kingdom, too. As we know, God is not having it! Your gift can cause Heavenly goodness or hellish damage. It's your choice. What will it be? As you treat your home, so should you treat your church home. If you want your home to be nice, so should you want your church home. Love the church and not a budget. The Lord says to delight in Him, and He will give you the desires of your heart. Please Him first in His Kingdom efforts and the benefits will be yours to enjoy! Not only will you be blessed by your giving, but others will be blessed by your gift.

Because Lucifer was over the music ministry of Heaven, creative people are the hardest people in the world to work with. The enemy wants to make sure that the things we do from his lost "department" are not pleasing to God, who is the Creator of it all; his goal is to use God's creation to spit in His face by dishonoring Him with pride.

Entitlement seems to come with the gift of singing. It's a common fact that if you are a famous singer, you are entitled to be treated a certain way. "How dare you treat me such a way? Do you not know who I am?" "I dare you not to consider me first!" "I can sing rings around you." "I'm the best at what I do." "It can't and won't be done without me!" "They did alright, but it would have been better if they had asked me." "I'll go and start my own group; who needs a church?" "I'll shut this whole thing down until you apologize." "It won't happen unless you ask me to do it." "I won't be assisting because your budget does not accommodate my gifting." These are just a few comments I've heard in the past. I'm sure you can list your own coming through the ranks. Use your discernment to identify the source. Ask yourself: Is it pride or humility influencing my decision? You determine the father of it. Entitlement, pride, boastfulness, harshness, grandness, puffed-up-ness all belongs to one father, satan. God takes no ownership of any of these traits. Mark 10:45 (TPT) says, *"For even the Son of Man did not come expecting to be served by everyone, but to serve everyone, and to give His life as a ransom price in exchange for the salvation of many."*

I love church. It's in me to love church just as I love my home. I want my church to have the best of *everything* I have! If I can give it, I'm giving. If I can sing it, I'm singing. If I can address anything by speaking, I'm speaking! It's my home and I'm giving my best. No one should have to pay you to take care of your home. Again, if there is a budget available to pay you at your home church, then Praise God, address it, and make arrangements to fit into their budget. By no means am I suggesting being taken advantage of, as some churches will. No, you should be able to have the opportunity to discuss a budget for your regular and repeated services. However, don't allow budgets or a pay scale to dictate the quality of your sharing. Always go above and beyond! Do more than what is asked, and God will bless you beyond your expectation!

Paul told the Corinthians he wasn't taking pay from them because he didn't want them to think the reason why he was with them was for compensation. Paul did not want anything to get in the way of his mission. He did not want to give them anything to talk about that would hinder his message and his relationship with them. Paul valued their souls! He wanted nothing he did to be a blemish on the work of the Holy Ghost. When the Holy Spirit reveals to you hindrances/blemishes in your ministry, adhere to His instructions to rid your works of them. Let there be no reason on your part for an unsuccessful mission. If God calls you to it, let Him do it! God has a way of compensating His called. Trust me, God pays!

I have said all this to say to you, make yourself available to assist your church, your spiritual home, in any way possible. When you take care of God's business, He has a way of taking care of yours that will astound you. Don't be so insistent on your way of thinking of compensation. Be obedient and open-minded to the things of God and watch God blow your mind. Eyes have not seen, nor have ears heard what the Lord has in store for you!

I have always loved the church I'm assigned to. It's a supernatural love given by God. My church becomes my local "Jerusalem," my holy site for worship. Being once married to military personnel, I had to learn to adjust and adapt to where I was. Wherever I was stationed, my first mission was to decorate my home and find a church! I've have always wanted a place to serve. Wherever God is glorified and worshipped corporately is where I want to be!

Nursing Home
Being raised around the elderly, I have always had an affinity for older people. I love their company, wisdom and humor. There's nothing in the world like sitting at the feet of

wise and witty elderly people. They tell you things that can save your life!

My mother's profession was as a senior citizens' director at a community center. Oftentimes, her members would be confined to nursing homes and we would travel to visit them. Mommy loved her people and so did I! I learned at an early age to visit the sick and shut-in and I continue loving it to this day.

One day while visiting a nursing home, I thought while singing to them, *"Why not have them sing to me? There must be a former church choir member in here somewhere."* I spoke to the activities director of that facility and was granted permission to start a nursing home choir and they loved it! I had a singing community group of young adults who would accompany me from time to time to assist with this "Senior Choir." The nursing home's staff was sooo supportive with our effort. They loved to see us coming; however, they thought it was their duty to inform us of the residents who lacked people skills. They wanted us to be aware of the mean ones. (LOL!)

There was one such lady named Mother Martin who claimed to hate everybody. The staff warned me to stay away from her because she was not compliant with anything or anybody.

Mother Martin was a little 4'11" fireball who became my welcomed challenge. I loved "loving the hell out of her," and I must say she was full of it! I would visit her before each choir rehearsal that was held in the fellowship hall of the nursing home. She would let me know that she liked me but no one else in that facility. I would laugh and tell her to behave!

I asked her to be a part of our effort because I was told her husband was a pastor and she was the choir director at her church. OMGOODNESS, why did I ask her about church? She raged from church hurt. The bitterness of her church experience had taken ahold of her and made her so mean that not even her children could deal with her. The staff told me when her family used to visit, she would turn them away and tell them not to come back. When I spoke to her about her family and she realized I knew a little of her history, she cussed me out and told me to get out! I couldn't believe that little old lady could speak such language. I stood there, shocked and amazed, while allowing her to finish. When she nodded her head in completion, I asked her if she was finished and she told me "Yes!" Suddenly the love of God gripped me, and everything became hilarious to me! I remember laughing at her being so mean! I couldn't stop laughing! She smiled and glared up at me with the one eye she had left (because her other eye had been shut due to an illness) and cracked up at me laughing at her and said, "You don't know when to quit. I done cussed you out and you still here, and you say you love me! What kind of fool are you? Stupid is who you are! Why don't you just leave me alone?" I responded, "Because I love you and there is nothing you can do about it! I know you're just trying to be mean. If I don't come and see you, who will?" She told me no one, but she was used to it being that way, and tried to convince me that's the way she wanted it.

I left her alone for a couple of weeks after one of her tantrums, and when she heard me across the hall she screamed, "Angela!!! Is that you? You better bring your a _ _ (*rear end*) over here to see me. I'm not kidding! Don't make me get up out of this bed. You better come and see me!" I went over to her room and fussed at her for screaming like that and she just laughed and said, "Well, it worked! You over here ain't cha?"

One time, one of the singers in my group, who was a funeral home director, came and passed out his funeral home business cards. Noooo! Mother Martin read his card with her one eye and looked up at him and said "You must think I'm a fool. Why, I oughta whip you for bringing this card up here." *(Please note I'm typing as a Christian because she used choice words that were not clean! LOL!)* I had to rush him out of the room for his safety! Mother was about to get up and charge at him! He was in shock, not realizing the harm or offense he had caused. To him, it was only business. He thought giving funeral service options was appropriate and was only offering his services. Let's just say it was the wrong place, wrong time, and wrong person!

Another time, I took my sister, Nuana, to sing to her. Because we look so much alike, Mother Martin swore we were sisters. I tried to convince her that that was not the case. She wouldn't change the subject to allow us to sing. She kept asking me, "Why can't you see this is your sister? I only got *one* eye and I can see that! Are you stupid? What's wrong with you?" I responded, "Mother Martin, she is not my sister. We are from different states. We are not blood related." She said, "Now, I know you are! I know you are! Y'all got the same father! I know it!" I argued, "No we don't. Her father is a bishop!" She shut the argument down when she said, "I don't care if he is a preacher! His d_ _ _ *(private part)* wasn't preaching!" *(OMG!! Exit stage left!!!)* Nuana's mouth flew open and I tried to save her by pushing her out the door! Mother Martin did not hold her tongue. If she thought it, she said it! I knew then that Mother Martin was a one-on-one ministry for me only, and for some reason, I believe she liked it that way. She would just look at the ceiling while I sang and hummed to her or read her a story.

I did convince her to participate in a program for Christmas that showcased our nursing home choir. After months of begging her to share her gift with the people, she finally consented to reading a Scripture to open the service. I was *sooo* proud and happy that she was going to be a part of this event because the staff had told me she *never* would. They were in shock to see her in a choir robe. We had borrowed robes from a local church and each nursing home choir member was able to be fitted and have one for the program. It was simply beautiful. Each one of my group members was responsible for processing a nursing home choir member to the "choir stand," which was from the back to the front of the fellowship hall. *Ohhhh...it was beautiful!* The nursing home choir sang as we pushed them in their wheelchairs to the beat of the music, just like days of old when a choir would "march in." They sang!!! The fellowship hall was full of family members and friends. It was sweet! I couldn't wait to showcase Mother Martin so that everyone could see the sweet side of her that I saw, and here we go...

We opened with prayer and a welcome. The choir sang their first number while processing in, after which Mother Martin was scheduled to read Scripture. This was my moment to prove that love conquers hate. She instructed her young "escort" to push her wheelchair over next to the artificial tree in the room, that was positioned in the front next to the podium. When she got in that position, she held on to the tree and I gave her a mic. My proud moment! *(Thinking...see I told you all she would act right.)* The staff went up in thunderous applause and I just cried. I was so proud! After a brief introduction, I leaned over to her and said, "Mother, it's time for you to read your Scripture. Do you have your Bible?" She said, "I don't need one. I memorized my verse." OMG! She went a step further and memorized it for us. This was joy unspeakable! She asked us if we were ready and I told her, "Yes mother, proceed!" She began by saying, "For God so loved the world that He gave His only begotten son." Now I'm beaming with tears streaming down my face, "Yes, Mother, yes! Yes He did!" She continued to say, "And what do we give Him? We don't give Him sh_ _!" *(BooBoo)*. I began to scream, "Oh no!!! Get her! She's cussing! Somebody grab her! Take the mic! She's cussing!" They tried to push her out, but she would not release the tree and kept shouting, "Let me go. Let me say what I wanna say! You dun' got me out here. Now let me say it my way, ya' hear!" She would not let go of that tree, and we ended up escorting her with the tree out of the fellowship hall while she cussed during her entire exit. The audience nearly fell out of their seats laughing, while some were shaking their heads and saying, "That's the truth, isn't it!" I was sooo outdone as I looked at the faces of the staff who silently said to me, "We tried to tell you." That was something to behold. I had never heard the Scriptures recited with cuss words. I never put her in that position again!

Mother lived about another year and called me her daughter. I was the relative they called upon her death. They buried her with an afghan I had crocheted for her, which she loved, along with her husband's too large house shoes that she refused to take off. I asked her one time why she wore those too-large men house shoes that got in the way of every-thing. She told me they were her husband's and they were the only thing she had left of his. She said her family took every-thing she had of his except those house shoes and she didn't trust anyone with them. No more questions were asked about those shoes she wore.

Singing at Home

Your worship at home prepares you for worship with others. Your devotion time is imperative to your craft. You can never take anyone where you've never been. If you are a worship leader, you can only lead your congregation to where you've been. You cannot expect to connect with God on stage if you do not connect with Him at home. He wants to meet with you without an audience. Without His presence, even singing is only entertainment. There is no power in entertainment. People will enjoy you, of course, but the supernatural will not happen in the realm of entertainment.

You must be connected to the Father before you hit the stage. You have to bring your worship with you. Be prepared to do it alone, because some choir members and worship team members are only there for entertainment. I don't understand how people can call it worship when they are doing everything and talking about everything *before* they hit the stage. *Ohhh!* I can't stand it! I have to listen to the Lord before I go on stage. Whatever it is you have to talk about can wait until after the service. Service times are God's sacred times. My desire is to do it right and you can only do it right if you hear from God. He tells you what needs to be done to lead, encourage, reveal, anoint and heal His people. You cannot allow unfocused behavior to get in the way of His leading.

You must understand that satan comes to steal your worship and the productivity of corporate praise. He hates one-accord worship. Your focus cannot be on other things prior to corporate worship and then expect the "one-accord" to begin when you hit the stage. No! Your time of tarrying, which is waiting on Him, begins when you get up in the morning and understand your duty for the day. The Scripture says, "And when they were in one accord…," meaning there was a time when they were *not*. We must become one in bringing our worship with us in order to execute a focused, uniform, and productive time of worship together with everyone. The congregation can feel your spirit when you open your mouth. It's a waste of time to worship Him *without* Him.

When you worship in the privacy of your home, it enhances your ability to hear from Him; then when you are away from home and it's time to lead, you will know His voice and hear His instructions on what to do to lead that particular audience. Only God knows what His people need. God's anointing trumps people's talent and self-exploitation every time!

When you are a true worshipper at home, work, church, and play, you can expect the unexpected. Anticipate God's leading every time. God is always at work! He will mark you with His approval and reveal Himself to others in your worship. He wants all to know that He is God. Even those who are mere spectators will witness His mighty presence during your time of worship.

A sinner will remember a song before he will remember a sermon. Why not show the unbeliever what happens when you believe? Why not allow the Lord to use you to win or lead a soul with your surrendered gift? How well can you prepare the atmosphere with your gift of singing for the infallible Word of God that is to be preached after you sing? How well do you present the Lord in a concert where there is no spoken Word, only your singing? How well do you showcase God and not yourself? You can showcase yourself, having no power, or showcase God who has all power. Why waste your time showcasing yourself and your talent? What will it do for your audience long-term? Nothing!

How you serve now determines your reward later. What will your reward look like? Paul said he'd been whipped, stoned, shipwrecked, sleepless, lied on, and hungry for the sake of the Gospel. What are we willing to do for the Gospel? Do we only want what the world has to offer us now or are we living to live again?

Singing at Funerals

Contrary to popular belief, funerals are to be a celebration for the saints. I believe this with all my heart. I believe in the cloud of witnesses. I believe in Heaven. I believe in the New Heaven and New Earth. It's so unfortunate that we don't celebrate the creative God He is. The same God who created the earth we enjoy today is the same God who promises a New Earth without blemish. The same God who founded family is the same God who will bring families together again. Allow me to say that He is the same God who introduced animals to Adam and who will reconnect you with yours and me with mine! *(Tiny and three Cinnabars, who are my beloved pets who are gone on, and now Precious!)*

We will enjoy the company of each other. The same cycle of life we experience now will only get better. Working, laughing, eating, creating, discovering, and companionship will be ours to enjoy. Did I forget to mention the mansions? Wow! He said, "I'm going to prepare a place for you." The God of the universe, who has proven Himself to you over and over and over again has told you that He's preparing a place for YOU! God has no budget limits and you don't have to be pre-approved for a mortgage loan for your mansion. It's for You! Just as He met the disciples on the seashore cooking fish for them after His resurrection, He is making preparations for You! *(Lord Jesus, You know I don't eat fish, but may I have chicken wing flats fried hard with lemon pepper, a Caesar salad with tomatoes, and a loaded baked potato, of which I'm sure you'll hold the bacon...? LOL.)* He wants us to enjoy what He has prepared and is preparing with you in mind! Saints of God, He has a place of utmost joy prepared for us!

We do such a disservice to Him when we don't express His creative qualities. We depict the most boring scenes of Heaven, with fat angels sitting on clouds holding harps. We depict anemic angels and monstrous demons. We give all the fun and power to satan and never teach the fact that everything, and I mean everything, he does is a counterfeit to the joys and the power of the Lord. There is no joy like Holy joy. There is no life like holy living. satan wants clubs full and churches empty. Now some churches are so boring that they ought to be empty. However, satan will keep dead and compromising churches open because he doesn't lose. People don't want to go to boring churches, and in compromising churches, peoples' lives are not changed, but instead they are encouraged to be their own, unrepentant selves. Either way, the depiction of God is tainted. We must understand that satan is so upset because he's been dispelled from the glories of Heaven. His goal is to make sure few enjoy thoughts of Heaven, where he once had the privilege to reside.

So, when you have the ministry opportunity to sing at a "Celebration of Life" *(a funeral)* for a Christian, do so as you know where the transitioned saint has gone. Ask the Lord to allow your time of ministry to be a time to give the family a glimpse of Heaven! No ministry times are wasted times, so ask God to use you every second. The love, joy and peace you bring to the service will be what the family will experience through you. Your personification of hope will exude by the anointing of the Holy Spirit!

When my mother left this earth for Heaven, she had left instructions for me to sing her favorite choir song, "The Battle Hymn of The Republic." It was something I did not want to do, but knew that I had to if I believed what I said I believed. Yes, the newfound separation was hard, but I had to celebrate her life as best I could, and this was her request.

Everyone expressed their sympathy and understood if I couldn't do it. Their condolences were real and thoughtful. They wanted to make sure I knew I could grieve and decline her request for me to sing, but how could I decline such a request when the songs I sang said, "When We All Get To Heaven," "Yes, God is Real," "It's a Highway to Heaven," "Holy People Heaven Belongs to You," "By and By When the Morning Comes," etc. I had been trained to send the saints home through music, and my mother was due the honor by the fruit of her womb, which was me. She had taught and prepared me to sing for everyone, and this included her!

The Indianapolis Christ Church choir accompanied me in singing her song with much fervor. When I sang the words, "His truth is marching on," I thought of all the truths she had taught me about the God she had introduced me to. My conviction was made sure, and I pledged to always be available to declare His truths as they would march on! I sang this over my mother's earthly remains and I believed every word I sung. I felt her dance to the song as I sang it. I felt her encourage me to declare this truth until I die, and this I do.

While reminiscing on ministering at funerals of people

who were close to me, my ex-husband's funeral was a little different. Through the years we became the best of friends because he wasn't my husband. LOL! God had rendered a supernatural ability to forgive that neither of us could explain. We literally loved each other as brother and sister. Wayne would call to check on John and I monthly. John and Wayne grew to love each other! They respected each other's place in my life and neither was threatened.

Wayne had married a few times after me before he met his last wife, Jennifer. OMGOODNESS! Jennifer is as sweet as can be. I love her. I would constantly thank her for taking care of Wayne and his hard head. *(Side note: It was the funniest thing at their wedding when he would introduce me to her family. He and Jennifer would be so proud to present me as his ex-wife to strangers. Their expressions were priceless as we loved on each other in front of them! I loved every minute of it!)*

During his last visit to the hospital, Wayne was out of control. No one could calm him and make him follow instructions. Jennifer reached out to me for help. She was simply spent. With John's permission, I drove five hours to Indianapolis to straighten him out! Wayne knew better and I needed to "remind" him.

When I arrived at the hospital, he was on the first floor and I heard him at the entry door of the hospital. He was cutting up so loudly! I followed the voice and decided to let the nurse finish what she was doing and not interrupt her. When I sensed she was packing up, I turned that corner and said, "Boy if you don't stop that noise, you better. Embarrassing us like this. This is not how we act." Wayne had forgotten they had amputated his foot and jumped out of the wheelchair screaming, "My ex-wife! My ex-wife!" The nurse looked so surprised. She then looked at Jennifer who was nodding "yes" with such a happy face that she hurried and got her things together while looking at us as if we all were crazy! Wayne obviously forgot the pain he was in and began to tattletale on everyone who had mistreated him there by not doing what he wanted them to do. Then he begged me for a chicken sandwich from Wendy's that he was not allowed to have because of the salt intake. He was craving salt while on dialysis. He wanted some salted foods and not hospital food! We laughed and laughed, and I was able to spend a few days with them.

It was shortly after this visit that Wayne passed. The funeral would be different because during his life, he insisted on not being the churchgoer. He hated traditional church and his wife honored his request to not have service at a church and had it at their clubhouse where they had hosted parties. Well, what am I to do with this as he requested me to sing, "Going Up Yonder," a church song? He had told me to quit singing all them old-fogey Mahalia Jackson songs and sing some new ones like, "Going Up Yonder," "Uncloudy Day," and "Oh, Happy Day." Mind you, this was in 2017. *(Really Wayne?! LOL!)*

I arrived at his celebration and it appeared to be a party going on. Balloons were everywhere, inside and out. The room was decorated with pictures everywhere. Everything about Wayne's life was displayed. Jennifer even showcased pictures of him and me. It was *sooo* sweet in that room that I felt a song was not necessary to lift anyone's spirit. I wanted everyone to continue to enjoy family. This was a party and not a service, and to turn the attention to a soloist would be anticlimactic. It just so happened that people began to share their stories about life with Wayne. I, the ex-wife, certainly had mine. Everyone shouted, "Okay, Angie, tell the truth! Give us some real stories about Wayne."

We laughed, loved, shared, and cried. After I spoke, I sung. I sang in celebration of him and in appreciation of the times he did share with me. I tell everyone I didn't leave him because I didn't love him, as we've always loved each other; we just had to figure out how. Just because you aren't with me doesn't make you my enemy. No, I can actually love you enough to let you go. God provides wisdom, strength and the ability to do things His way. I left that clubhouse feeling complete. This was another chapter of my life closed by using a singing gift God has given me to serve mankind.

Still Waters: The Christian Light Club

It was God's idea. It was designed to be a safe place for the saints to go for clean fun and entertainment. I teamed up with my husband to create such a forum for Christians. We were both active in our churches. Just finishing ministry school at our church, we would sing in the choir from time to time. We wanted to do more for those around us. Together, we seem to have fun that others enjoy, and we are a natural team for entertainment. We both can work each other's nerves and it's funny! We decided to share the gift of song and laughter that we had. All our lives we watched Red Skelton, Foster Brooks, Flip Wilson, and my favorite, The *Carol Burnett Show*. I was inspired by the much-loved *Carol Burnett Show* to bring clean fun to those who aspire to live holy lives. I wanted it to be a place where even God could laugh and enjoy us having fun. A place where you could be pampered by hosts, and entertained by, not just Christian music, but also by some carefully selected secular songs. We chose and prayed over secular songs that were lyrically correct and life-giving that prompted the gift of joy for the strength of the saints. It was a time of wonderful food and talent in all creative ways, such as singing, poetry, drama and dance. We started out as a monthly show with new entertainment every show. *Ohhh my goodness*; this was a lot of work!

We had to fill the show every month to reach a budget to pay the workers. We had a select few entertainers and backstage workers. Our cast normally consisted of 6-8 singers, a comedian, a dramatist, and an 8-piece live band. I tried to stay true to a fun, clean and safe variety show. I knew that the enemy would use any space given him to pervert anything; therefore, I stayed on guard at all times with an eye of an eagle! It was work, but well worth it for the sake of the enjoyment of the saints. With Tim Conway and Carol Burnett as my inspiration, there was nothing too silly that we would not try!

Ms. Puddin'

Ms. Puddin' (Gale Mayes) was the show's Tim Conway. She would make laughter hurt. You never knew what was coming out of her mouth! She could say anything and get away with it because she played the role of an old lady, and as you know, the elderly can get away with speaking their thoughts. She would let us have it with her dry humor! I would attempt to keep things "holy," and she'd let me have it. She'd let me know, continuously, that I was not her boss and she could do what she wanted to do and that she and God were the best of friends! There was nothing I could say to correct her! She was a comedian who heckled the audience, and they loved it! She would ask a woman in the audience, "Why is your husband looking at me? He must want me!"

Then the lady would die laughing while the man sat there not knowing where to hide!

Ms. Puddin' would take current news and events and wrap it up in her humor in a way that would have you leaving with a totally different perspective than when you came. She was our gospel "Rona Barrett!" She had a way of making you laugh about life and its most difficult situations.

Once, she said she now had proof that Michael Jackson was, indeed, black, because white folk won't allow their dead to stay out' the ground more than two days! She said, "We black folk hold our people out' the ground so long, we forget they dead!" We all died laughing!

Ms. Puddin' was famous for her "lawnmower" dancing and her singing. She is a writer of songs that are totally ridiculous such as, "Jesus Is My Cousin" and "The Devil Pushed Me Down the Stairs!" We loved to hear her sing with all her facial expressions, body movements and flamboyant costumes. She declared a reunion with her singers called The Puddinaires. Y'all, from the moment she hit the stage, laughter hit the air! She invited her old singers to rejoin her one last time, her last tour with her singers. Her singers hit the stage as flamboyant as she was, and just crazy! It was like they were all freed from an asylum. One singer was a "floor roller" who would hit the floor rolling when she got happy in the "spirit" *(let me say it wasn't the Holy Spirit!)*. Another singer was so happy and hopped all over the stage excitedly and never completed a sentence. One singer came in with blue hair and eyes wandering into space looking for Ray Charles because she sung with him! The last singer, who had died just before the show, had her morticians to bring her to her last gig, and they walked her in in a casket. They put the casket stage front until Ms. Puddin' advised them that she was a background vocalist and belonged in the back. We hollered again! They picked up this casket that John Primm had sooo cleverly built for the show and hoisted that casket right on to the back of that stage! *And boy did they sing!* They were all professional singers who joined together singing "All Night, All Day Angels Watching Over Me." OMG! It was *wonderful!*

Denise Marcia

Denise was our dramatist, stage manager, and host for the evening. People would just come to be lifted by her smile and her attention. Everything backstage was always in order. There was never "dead air" in her presence. Everything had a purpose and a place, and if you were not in yours, let's just say she would graciously remind you to get in it! She didn't play when it came to order, no ma'am! Denise was driven to get things done right and timely. Shoot, John and I were the founders and she had no problem with putting us in our place if we were out of it! Do you understand what I'm trying to say? Hearing her voice from a distance made you ask yourself, "Now what am I supposed to be doing so that she doesn't have to remind me?"

She is gifted in the arts of drama and dance. She was magnificent in every character role she played, and there were many. We would discuss a portrayal idea and begin to write the monologue, and we had no limits! Every piece written was a masterpiece full of information and wisdom for the listener.

My favorite performance by her was a tribute to the plight of Harriett Tubman during Black History Month. My feeling was that we never acknowledge our white brothers and sisters who also gave their lives for the freeing of the slaves. Denise played the role of a white-faced Southern Belle who willingly became an underground conductor after meeting, in the town's general store, a woman named Harriett Tubman, affectionately called "Black Moses." The Southern Belle told of her story from stage right while smoke filled stage left. At the end of her monologue I began to sing "There's A Place for Us" from *Westside Story*. And dancer, Joy Young, who was playing Harriett Tubman, entered and curtsied to the Southern Belle who returned the gesture; they then embraced each other and danced together. Ohhh my; there was not a dry eye in the house!

Mike-E

There was another person I could count on to forget himself to become whoever we needed for the month and entertain God's people with all he had. His name is Mike-E. What a joy he was to the club. He would even entertain the people outside, prior to their entering the building, by portraying a black Barney Fife who "policed" the area where they parked. He would give grief to all who came and make them laugh about it! His costume had a gut that was as large as he was tall! He didn't strap a gun, but he did carry one bullet in his pocket to threaten you if you parked wrong, according to him. It was a mess and people loved it!

Whatever Mike-E was asked to do, he did it, no matter how ridiculous. While playing the soulful role of B.B. King, he sat on that guitar, "Lucille," and you swore it was B.B. playing her! Then came Chuck Berry! OMG! He skidded across that stage, slinging his wig while playing "Johnny B. Goode." The place erupted with joy and Mike-E's back was out for two weeks! When he hit the stage in his purple suit, ruffled white shirt, and platform shoes, all it took was one chord of "Purple Rain" and the saints would lose it! I would laugh out loud at how much the saints would cut up and how they knew these songs that I had to google! How did the saints know so much about this secular stuff?! Mike-E is a clown and loves to clown around. He was such an asset to our bank of fun! He never surrendered an opportunity to bring laughter, no matter what he had to do.

John Primm

I am noted for being the background vocalist; however, my husband, John, holds his own in music. He portrayed everyone from Cab Calloway to Nickolas Ashford. John is crazy! He and I planned to sing "Solid as A Rock" on this particular show. I was to start the song and he would join me. Listen, y'all! When he came out on stage, John had on a glistening black shirt with a dripping jheri curl wig and shoulders pads that were taller than he. I died on stage! I had no clue he was doing this, and I was not prepared for the surprise. I could not suppress my laughter to sing the song! All I could do was cry and laugh at the same time while trying to figure out his costume. I was in shock! I couldn't believe he had snuck this in on me. No one warned me, not even Denise. I wanted to ask him why he thought this stunt was necessary. I tried to apologize to the audience for losing control and ask for their patience to get to and through the song. They were so busy laughing at us, which only made me laugh harder! We were all out of control and he kept asking me, "What's-a-matter, baby? Why are you not singing, baby?" in an Ashford smooth style, which only loosened my grip to any order I so desperately needed to continue the show. John only made things worse with a false innocence he portrayed while looking ridiculous! I wanted to scold him because of this surprise. He knew we had a tight show for the evening, and no time was allotted for "unscheduled" foolishness! The audience and I could not pull it together. I tried to sing, but only laughter was released as he looked at me *sooo* seriously. He had his part together and was singing! He never broke a smile! Even after the song, he simply swayed off the stage as I looked on in amazement and tried to host the rest of the show. I was never able to pull it back in. I was tickled the rest of the night; this was hilarious!

People love hearing John imitate Louis Armstrong. He has him down packed perfectly! Even now when we travel on the road, people in church ask for John to sing "What A Wonderful World." People love John. He did Rufus Thomas' song, "Walking the Dog" in full garb, including the cape and boots. When the band played the introduction to this song, the people knew it, and John came out "barking" and singing! We had a husband and wife team who danced in costume, with him being in a giant dog costume and her in poodle skirt attire. It was wonderful and John, again, was ridiculously wonderful! I love my husband to pieces with his crazy self!

John Primm as Rufus Thomas

Still Waters' Challenges

Even though Still Waters was God's idea, we faced many challenges. I had to know and believe that God had called me to it. We faced many location problems. Within the 14 years the show ran, we had to move five times due to budget restraints as owners increased rental prices and refused to make repairs to their buildings when needed. There had to be an open space for tables, chairs, and a stage that could hold a cast crew of up to 20 people at a time. With a following of approximately 400 people, we had to perform two shows to accommodate everyone because our largest room could only seat approximately 250 at a time. For locations that didn't have tables and chairs, we had to provide them, set them up, tear them down and load up after each show. This became problematic for "old" workers, such as my husband. It was extremely laborious. Each location had its own set of issues, but the testimonies of how the saints were blessed made it worth it! People would come heavy-laden and leave lightly burdened. There were people who came after leaving a funeral; they didn't want to miss the fun of the evening! It was sooo sweet! One pastor's testimony was that he reneged on his thoughts of divorce after a show where John and I sang to each other "Endless Love." Wonderful testimonies poured in after each show. This was rewarding to us all.

There were many challenges entertaining Christians. Some Christians didn't think fun was appropriate for Christian living. Some didn't like the carefully selected secular music for a Christian stage. They complained that even with these chosen songs it was still too "churchy." I understood that a saint can't sing everything that's popular. Boy, did I have my fights over this! There were some who were upset because I would not allow the singing of some favorite songs that were not Christian stage worthy. I didn't care how popular the song was, you were not singing about "Me and Mrs. Jones" or "Wait 'Til the Midnight Hour." No sir, not on my watch. Some patrons stopped coming because they didn't like the idea of an altar call at the end of each show. They stated if they wanted to go to church, they would do just that and not have to buy a ticket.

Some didn't understand why we didn't serve alcohol. We had opportunity for festive dancing, but not groping. We would adhere to family line-dancing and *Soul Train* lines that were safe. I would watch carefully, as there were people, and some unknowingly, who would come and try to cross the line; however, with love, I would pull them from the line to "calm them down" and explain to them where they were. By the grace of God, no love was ever lost, and we loved everyone through every would-be misunderstanding. We had Christian standards and did not compromise.

Hospice and Funeral

There was a wonderful, sweet lady, whose name was Ms. Gloria, that had patronized us for many years who was diagnosed with cancer. As her health declined, all she wanted to do was get to the show to laugh. We made arrangements to have her transported with her bed to the show, and she loved it! We so enjoyed having her there and loved on her all night during the show. OMG! She laughed all night!

When it became too risky to move her, we went to visit her in her hospice facility. Her favorite was Ms. Puddin'. Ohhh, she got a kick out of Gale! Ms. Puddin' showed up and fussed over her and threatened everyone who had a hand in her care, including the doctors, while winking her eyes at them all the while. Ms. Gloria was sooo tickled! She hadn't said anything in weeks and then all of a sudden, she mustered up, "Get 'em Ms. Puddin." The room went up in laughter and all I could do was cry.

We were requested by the family to sing the show's closing song, "I'm Going to Be Ready" at her funeral, and we did. It was a blessing to be chosen to bring lightness to such a dire situation. We loved her and she knew it. We were there and she knew it!

Receiving Lines

This is where individual ministry began. We, the performers, at the end of each show, would line up at the exit doors to thank our guests for coming. In these "receiving lines," we prayed together, laughed together, and sometimes cried. These lines were filled with tears and hugs. We understood the importance of touch, and that sometimes we were releasing people to a world of hard decisions; we wanted no one to feel alone.

People traveled far to attend, some as far away as Texas. We would go the extra mile to love on everyone and inform each attendee that they were special. This was the job of Still Waters. God's people treated royally. It was truly our pleasure.

CHAPTER 5

BACKGROUND VOCALIST FOR TELEVISION AND FOR LIVE SHOW TAPINGS

I have shared with you my beginnings as a professional singer singing on the *Bobby Jones Gospel* television show. But as time progressed, God had plans for other television and live taping opportunities. When you serve the Lord, you can never anticipate the opportunities He has for you. For Him to be able to use you effectively, your heart must be in the right place; otherwise, you will not be able to discern whether God or satan is using your gift. satan has plans for your gift too and desires to use them, and he does! You must understand and settle in your spirit that every good opportunity is not of the Lord. satan knows how to set you up with enough good opportunities to cause you to fail, for this is his goal for your gift and your life. Comply only with the Lord and never compromise with the devil.

There is a major difference in singing live—such as on television, on DVD tapings, or on stage—than singing in the studio. You must prepare for it differently. The studio allows you the opportunity to retake the song, while a live performance is what it is—live. Sometimes in live recordings, you are allowed a "retake" that directors can use in an editing process, and this is great; however, you are expected to know your materials.

The pay scale for a live performance differs from a studio performance. A studio normally pays by the hour or per song, whichever is greatest. In live performances, you are paid for your performance, no matter how long it takes during the day. A television taping can be an entire-day process.

One year, I did a television show in Hollywood, CA that paid $1,200.00 for a two-minute spot. Because we singers hadn't joined the union, everyone's check was kept to pay their dues to the union except mine. *Why? What happened?* Well, I was able to get a full check in the mail because they had misprinted my social security number and couldn't find me in their system to determine whether or not I paid my dues. They had it wrong and I didn't correct them. I took my check and ran! *(LOL!)* You have to be able to afford the fees of the union and they are expensive. I have never been fortunate to have enough "union scale" work to deem union fees necessary.

Gale and I had a background gig to sing on the television show, *The Voice.* It was a two-day gig that paid for a one-song TV appearance and a concert afterward. Later, we found out that each gig for this short Los Angeles tour paid separately. It was a blessing!

There are television shows that only offer exposure, which are just as important when you are trying and needing to convey a gospel message. You cannot disregard the unpaid for the paid. You must know what you are called to do and the importance of sharing the gospel with your gift. All television programs are important. Television can reach the masses at one time. It's a blessing from the Lord to have such an opportunity to do so. Say "yes" to all media of communication. Don't sit on your gift for paying gigs only. Allow the Lord to use your gift with or without pay. The Lord knows your needs and He will provide!

Gaither Video Tapings

For over 20 years, I have been a studio singer for Bill Gaither. When he desires a particular sound for a particular song, he knows who to hire to make it happen. Gale and I have been his Black Gospel background singers for years.

Bill Gaither hosts numerous video series for his audience that have been successful throughout the years. Gale and I have been privileged to be his guests on many of them. We are so blessed! His office will contact you to inform you of the song(s) you will lead or sing background vocals for. Prior to internet, you were sent CDs of the music for the entire evening, but now you receive downloadable MP3s. It's amazing!

Upon arriving at the studio for the taping, I greet, speak, hug and kiss, and then prepare my mind for worship. The fellowship that takes place with Gaither's various artists is overwhelmingly sweet. Bill and Gloria would have it no other way. There is to be no negativity or complaining on the set. Unspoken instructions are to: 1. Know your music 2. Love your music 3. Love each other—not necessarily in that order, but this is expected with zero tolerance for anything else.

Different tapings have different themes, and he has an audience awaiting every video released. He is trusted by his audience to produce what they love, and with excellence, and he never disappoints.

I've been blessed to be a part of many Bill Gaither videos. I'm *sooo* grateful for all the opportunities to be with my Gaither family. There is no feeling like it in the gospel industry. Let me try to put this in words. Working for a person who is not in need makes all the difference in the world. Bill Gaither has no need to be affirmed, and neither does Gloria. God has affirmed them in His work. Both are settled in the things of God and are working at making miracles happen for The Kingdom. God showed them what He needed them to do, and they struck out and did it! On the other hand, when you work for someone who is desperate to be recognized, heard, affirmed, and worshipped, you will find yourself paying for their low self-esteem and narcissistic ways with your sanity. You will be left trying to figure out what you could have done better, given more of, or helped more with. You can never satisfy a narcissistic person. I'm sad to say that narcissism is an illness that is prevalent among singers, and this fact does not exempt gospel artists. When they feel as if they aren't "observed" by you enough, you quickly become their enemy.

I have never, in all my years of working with Bill Gaither, felt this type of demonic pull from him, his staff, or his artists. When your foot hits the set to begin a time of ministry with his organization, you are immediately loved by him, organized by his staff, and celebrated by other artists. I've never witnessed or experienced such love and sweet fellowship from an organization that has the responsibility of so many artists on one set. It is always a family reunion when we gather.

I sit back and observe how the entire enterprise is run. It begins from the call inviting you, to the prepping praise and worship, to how we are escorted on and off by the staff to minister. Please allow me to say this: During live performances with audiences, Bill even has a staff that lovingly and strategically organizes your product tables to ensure that "everyone is a winner," as Bill so graciously and often says.

Each videotaping with Gaither is so special. We are told dress themes and the music to study. There is absolutely no greater gathering than with spiritual "parental" leadership, and the saints as your "siblings." There is simply no greater gathering on this earth. However, I do have my favorites.

"Precious Lord, Take My Hand"

There was one particular time we were scheduled to tape on Billy Graham's campus. We traveled on a bus and were having a wonderful time when all of a sudden, at the entrance of the campus, we all began to speak in hushed and reverential tones. We were in awe of the sudden sweet presence of the Holy Spirit. It was *amazing*! We could all feel the presence of Jehovah in that place.

When we realized what had happened, we looked at each other and laughed! It was the strangest thing. Everyone did it subconsciously. We were on holy ground and our minds, without telling us, knew it. Even in our joy during the day, there was a hushed reverence that permeated the atmosphere where we were. Billy Graham's anointing, even though he was not in our presence, was all over the place. That place is a place of prayer!

We had been asked to choose attire that would honor the 1920's-40s. It was a wonderful time of preparation. It was a time I could dress as ladylike as I wanted with gloves, hat, and all. I loved it!

Bill informed me to prepare to sing the second verse to "Precious Lord, Take My Hand." I did and ad-libbed out on the ending chorus. When I finished and loved on "Momma" Gloria's shoulder as I love to do when concluding a song when she is present, I heard "Daddy" Bill continue the song. *Okay...this is fine, as we sometimes repeat a chorus to include the audience. But wait a minute—wait one minute! He's handing the mic to Jason Crabb?! This was not going to remain a quiet moment as it had been! Lord No! Not Jason! That boy is as Pentecostal as they come! Let me get out of the way of this fire! I sought shelter and tried to duck in my seat.* Bill walked directly toward me with the mic. *NO!!! I plead the 5th! I have no dogs in this fight! I have not a nickel in that quarter! Please don't hand me the mic! I'm feeling the Holy Ghost!* I looked down at Gloria and she smiled at me with her wonderful motherly expression that said: "proceed daughter." By that time, Bill was in front of me instructing me to answer Jason's call in the song.

OHHH NOOO—I'm fired!
Well, I did answer Jason back in the song with the passion for the message that had taken over. I knew I risked the chance of being misunderstood, because the song had turned "left" and we were going "right!" God took complete control! Not knowing what Bill truly wanted, I just gave him what I had. I prayed, "Lord, I know how we do this, but I'm in a different audience Jesus! Lord, I need Your help! This call and answer technique is common in the Black Gospel genre,

but we are taping in front of a nearly all-white audience here. Lord, they are going to hate me!" But it was too late...it had been done. Next thing I hear is Jason Crabb saying, "You finish it!" As much as I tried to suppress it, our wires had been connected by Bill. *Booyyyeee*, the sparks flew, the battery was charged and the engine revved! It was a moment totally out of man's control.

Nothing had been planned and it worked for The Kingdom. I learned they didn't hate me for it but embraced me because of it. As of 2020, there are more than 28 million views of this video on YouTube. People share their testimony with me of how this song ministers to them and some watch it daily! When I travel to minister, people have wanted to try to recreate this moment, but it's impossible to do because it was a moment created by the Father. It was not and cannot be planned. It's just one of those things God did for His people. God orchestrates moments of ministry that have nothing to do with the vessel He chooses to use. As Bill Gaither says, *"Why not?!"*

"Said I Wasn't Gonna Tell Nobody"

I loved my mother so much, and this song I recorded of hers was one she led with her Mothers and Daughters chorus. I recorded it and Bill loved it! It's a simple call and answer song. It's a song of lively testimony that the audience loves. Everywhere I go, someone has watched the video that Bill produced and wants to recreate this moment. Again, it's impossible to recreate that moment, but we certainly have our own wherever I go!

I was called by his office to record this song on his next videotaping. I thought, *How sweet of him to ask me to do*

Mommy's song! Of course, I'll do it. It's a simple and short song. This should be easy enough, and I'll be able to share Mommy's song with my family. How sweet this will be for my family to go down memory lane!

Well, the Holy Ghost had His unscripted way in that place. I heard the way Bill Gaither said, "Angie Primm" at the end of my singing. I knew he meant to sing it another round. So, I took off in the freedom of the Holy Ghost, knowing they would have the ability to edit the tape for the final video. We had fun that evening and danced on that set like nobody's business. I tried to duck to my place beside my husband as to not disturb the audience any longer with the song, and then I felt the anticipation from the audience for another round!

At the beginning of the song I said, *"This is for you Mommy!"* because she would totally lose herself in this song of praise. I desired to mimic her excitement and joy for that audience and the taping! What happened at this taping must have been what happened to her when she would sing this song. Mommy would sing and shout her wig off during this song. Without missing a beat, she would reach down and pick up her wig and place it back on her head backwards! *(Most embarrassing moments of my childhood! MOMMY?! REALLY?!)* I remember wondering why on earth she felt the need to continue singing this song in such a terrible state. The short, fuzzy part of the back of the wig would showcase her forehead, while the huge and heavy front of the wig hung on the back of her neck. She had to feel that! She just had to realize that something was wrong but didn't care! Why did she feel the need to embarrass her children like this? After our time of ministry, I would feel the need to minister to her about the way she conducted herself and the securing of her wig if she was to act like this. She would always reply "You are not going to shame me into suppressing my praise. I'll praise Him how I want to. I'm the mother and you are the child. Maybe one day you'll have a praise like David and don't care what others think about you." Well needless to say, I'm like my mother. Now I don't shout my wigs off because I know better. I simply have mine sewn on! *(Now take that devil! LOL!)*

I was totally lost in the moment of this song of my mother, and the band and the Lee Singers joined right in with this glorious reprise; we had a ball singing God's testimony of praise. Like the song said, we couldn't keep it to ourselves and we didn't! What a time we had!

The Huckabee Show

Trè Corley is a wonderful producer whose family owns their own studio. I have worked with Trè for years in his studio laying tracks for people and Christian television shows. Trè called a few years ago to ask me if I was available to sing for a new television show. He wanted to know if I was interested in doing something like this on a regular basis.

My response to his request was yes. I am now contacted regularly for this television show when certain artists are scheduled and need background vocalists. We are sent the "demo" (demonstration of how the song is sung), and we study the song and our individual part before we meet corporately for a rehearsal and then the television taping. It's a *blessing* to be called and fun to work with my claimed "son," Trè Corley, and his family! We have a blast!

Replacement Singers

I received a call from someone who asked if Gale and I were available to do a live show at the Grand Ole Opry that evening. I called Gale to check her availability and she was available. She asked me who we were singing for. I told her I wasn't sure, but believed the caller said "Dooney and Bourke." Gale asked, "Angie, isn't that a purse?" I didn't know. I just remembered the name of the person who called me and figured we'd get the details later. Gale was so tickled!

We arrived backstage to meet up with the manager who introduced us to the artist we were singing for. It was Brooks and Dunn. Gale laughed so loudly in their faces upon introduction and proceeded to tell on me! Now everybody is laughing because I have called them "Dooney and Bourke," a purse! She is lowdown like that.

We did not know their music and they were not worried. They had hired us for stage presence only because their regular background vocalist was drunk and needed help pulling this show off. *What?!* Gale and I spent the evening trying to get parts to sing from their drunk singer to perform with her on stage. It was nerve-racking and funny! Gale can make anything funny! We literally stood on each side of her to hold her up while we sung on camera. After the performance, they went on and on about how grand it was while their singer was passed out on the couch. They liked it, so we loved it! It paid and we went home! LOL!

Drinks on The House

There was an artist Gale and I had sung for in the studio who hired us for a live performance taping. Sound check was at 11:00 a.m. and the show began at 7:00 p.m., with a rehearsal in between. He scheduled dinner for everyone and announced that drinks were on the house for anyone who desired to stay the entire day. Gale and I stayed the day because we can entertain each other. We love being in the company of one another and we discussed the songs, the show, and people in the band who were drinking all day!

Show time…the bass player is lit! Gale was hitting me while singing and saying under her breath, "Look, look, look. Angie, *look*!" The bass player was so drunk he was staggering and moving toward the lead singer's mic. He sung in the mic with the artist, who then directed him back to the band. By now, Gale and I are in shock! When the player was moved backward, he lost his balance and fell into the drums. This was all on tape! Stagehands assisted him quickly, but to our surprise, he couldn't stand up straight. He swayed every time he struck a chord. One chord played, then he swayed as if he had built a house—just proud of himself!

It was funny but terrible. This artist had spent all this money on a taping he could not use. It was ruined.

CHAPTER 6
BACKGROUND VOCALIST ON THE ROAD (STAGES & CHURCHES)

The Lord, aware of my love for church and my faithfulness to my call at home, saw fit to entrust me with opportunities on the road and abroad. Not everyone is so privileged, and I'm deeply grateful to Him for trusting me with His people. I pray I never disappoint the Lord with these precious opportunities to share His love through song, words, and hugs! I have one opportunity at a time to sing and say what "thus says the Lord" and sit down! If I should begin to shine the light on myself, the anointing would lift and I would be like the naked Emperor, showing his tail while his talent has him believing he is clothed.

Freedom Tour
Through the years, I have worked with wonderful artists in the studio and on the road. It's a wonderful feeling knowing your part and traveling to perform it.

This particular tour was called "The Freedom Tour," featuring Patti Austin. This woman was so powerful in her presentation. *I loved it!* We had to learn popular songs of freedom, even some in an African language. I was with the best of singers during this tour who assisted me all the way. It was quite intimidating and challenging, but the producer had faith in me and insisted that I learn. With rehearsals, it turned out to be a fantastic show and experience!

We had toured several cities in the States and had arrived in San Francisco. The singers could sense the unrest with the orchestra but had no idea what was happening. After our director, Sanchez Harley, rehearsed the rhythm section, he called a meeting for the leaders. The orchestra was dismissed and so were the singers. Our lead singer informed us what was discussed at the meeting.

Once the conductor of the San Francisco orchestra saw that the director was a black man, he refused to perform under his leadership. Sanchez made the decision to conduct the orchestra himself. We had no idea he had these skills, but he did; he is a genius! It was a jaw-dropping moment in rehearsal to see him take the reins and drive that pony home. We were in awe! This man rolled up his sleeves and conducted us all. I was so proud to know him and hear Patti bellow about "Freedom." It changed my life forever. Everyone seemed to have a different, new perspective about themselves while performing the next several shows. We entered the stage differently with a newfound determination. The atmosphere was triumphantly charged. Our purpose had become clearer, more distinct. Our banner had changed from them to "*we*." Don't cry about spilt milk; mop it up and keep moving to get another glass! That is what was done before our very eyes! YES!

The Wave

My most profound worship experience, as a background vocalist, was with worship leader and now pastor, Lindell Cooley. It was a time of worship at a woman's conference hosted by Judy Jacobs. The atmosphere was charged by her famous "Indian" warfare praise.

Gale, Melinda Doolittle, and I were hired to be the background vocalists for this event. Knowing Lindell, we knew to prepare for a time of high-strung praise because he has no inhibitions when it comes to worshipping the Lord, ministering the message, and ushering in His presence! NONE! Lindell hits the stage wanting all the Lord has to give! He would go from playing the keys, directing the band, instructing the singers, to running, skipping, jumping, laughing and crying! If he sensed the Holy Spirit's pleasure on a particular chord, he would write a lyric to go with that chord immediately and stay there until the Lord moved beyond it. He knows how to handle a time of worship like none other. It was as if the Lord would be standing by anxiously awaiting his praise to Him to join in with him! You just had to be ready and understand he was following the Lord at all costs. There were no "wait-a-minute-let-me-get-it-together" moments! Whatever he hears God say do at that moment, he does!!!

With the three of us black girls—who were professional background vocalists with innate style, rhythm, and dance—we knew we could hold it down gracefully.
We knew how to be emotional, yet professional. We were determined to hold this time of worship together with our professional selves. In other words, it doesn't take all of that; calm down!

This particular day at the Opryland Hotel, we had gathered backstage and had coached each other to be prepared for this time of worship with Lindell and Judy. This was going to be a powerful exhibit of the amazing manifestation of God's glory! It promised to be because both of these praise leaders were crazy for God! We were ready! *So, we thought!* We positioned ourselves and the praise began. It was wonderful as usual. But nothing, and I mean *nothing*, could have prepared us for what was about to happen.

We did our part and God did His and we were pleased and finished. *NOT!* Lindell left his keyboard, snatched his mic and danced toward us to inform us that we were not finished. He spoke into the mic that God was about to do something in the audience. We three girls looked at each other in relief because it had to do with the audience and not us! *Whew!* He introduced to them this thing called "The Wave." I, not knowing what he was talking about, looked to Gale for clarity, who shrugged her shoulders to tell me she had no clue. But her intense look seemed to say she knew something of it. Her facial expression went from "I don't know" to "Uh-ohhh!" I watched him instruct the audience to sit down and allow the back row to stand and sit, then the next row to stand and sit consecutively until the front row was finished. This was called The Wave. *(What?! Now I'm thinking only my white brothers and sisters would do such a thing, and why?! LOL!)*

He instructed the instrumentalists to play and us to sing. The back row began, and you could immediately feel the presence of the Lord. Now I'm in shock and was wondering what was happening! By the middle row, people behind them were passing out because of His powerful presence. Melinda began her nervous giggles and Gale was shaking her head "No." With each row, the power became mightier! I understood, with my simple mind, that by the time it reached the front, we would be in trouble! Melinda's giggles turned to full-on laughter as The Wave approached. Gale's nods went to a ducked head, and my eyes were wide with amazement and I could not shut my mouth! It's COMING! IT'S COMING!! HOLD ON!!! HERE HE COMES!!!

The Wave hit and we hit the floor! It was such a surge that even the most reserved person present could not have withstood its power. It felt as if we had been run over by a massive ocean wave. While on the floor, I could barely raise my head under such power, and I could still hear Melinda's laughter even louder. But where was Gale? Not able to raise my body or head entirely because of the weight of the anointing, I shifted my head to the side to see if I could see her. She was laying there beside me, prostrate! To know Gale, you must understand that she does none of this in or out of church. She always reminds me that she is Baptist, and she doesn't carry-on as such. I called her name to make sure she was okay. She turned her head to face me, still unable to lift it directly and said, "It knocked my shoes off and I need a pedicure!" I SCREAMED! After all that, all she thought about was her feet! She and the Holy Ghost, I could no longer handle! Where the Holy Ghost had so graciously laid me, I remained amazed, outdone, and just laughed! *Hmm,* that's all I could do under the weight of His precious presence.

No Showers and No Food
I had never in my entire singing career been on a tour where food and showers were not provided. It was scary. We literally had to get off the bus and walk to find souvenir shops in the area to purchase souvenir towels to bathe in the

locker room of that venue for the evening. There were other stops where we were expected to share one hotel room for eleven people (men and women) to shower. We had to ask management for cleaning supplies to take showers after so many people. For our survival, we took matters into our own hands. We began to reserve our own rooms and asked to stop at food chains and grocery stores to purchase food for the journey. We didn't know what each venue had in store for us, or should I say didn't have in store for us.

There were some stops that had *no food*. One time we were parked at a hotel in such a rural area where you couldn't even order pizzas. No one delivered in that area. Then we were told to eat at the hotel, only to find out that they only served breakfast that ended at 9:00 a.m. and it was 2:00 p.m.! Can anybody say, "Just *stuck*!"

The artist felt we were being ungrateful because his management had done the best they could with the budget that was provided for the tour. We were in shock that nothing had been prepared for us as a team. This was unheard of for any artist who traveled with a band and singers. It was clear this tour did not have our wellbeing in mind.

I couldn't wait to get home and regroup. By this time, I had been "BGVing" for over twenty years and had never experienced such treatment. *Where were they doing this at?* If this was the new norm, then normal me out. I was cussed out because I needed to lock a door to change clothes. I had never surrounded myself with such vile talk and couldn't understand what landed me there. When I asked if I could use the back of the bus to change my clothes, which is usually the artist's area, he looked up at me in his frustration and stated, "I don't give a f_ _ _ where you change clothes." I stood there looking at him, in shock, wondering, "What did you just say?" I remember getting off the bus after the tour ended, feeling numb. I felt as if I had been run over by a truck. I loved this artist so much and we'd shared wonderful times together for years. I never saw this coming. And I didn't ever want to see it again. My heart was broken. I knew something had to change. If my boss felt it was okay to speak to me in such a manner, then it was time to find another boss.

A few days after I returned home from this abusive tour, I heard the voice of God ask me, "Now, will you be a background vocalist for Me?" My spirit leaped and I totally surrendered my way of thinking in working as a BGV and said "Yes!" I had no idea of the turn of events that were about to take place.

I'm Gonna Take You on the Road

I was hired to be a BGV for a live recording of a DVD. Bill Gaither happened to be in the audience. He witnessed my stage presence and my ability to lead and fall into the background. After the show, he approached and said, "You're good, kid. I'd like to take you on the road with me sometimes." Then he walked away.

I didn't understand exactly what he meant, but I'm always looking for the next gig. So, whose music did I need to study to be prepared for going on the road? I cornered him during the reception following the recording and asked, "Bill, you mentioned me going on the road. Whose music am I needing to study? Who are you thinking of pairing me with?" He replied, "You, kid. You're good." Okay, I realized I wasn't making any progress here. I decided to just call his office in the morning, which I was familiar with from being called through the years in scheduling me for his video tapings. I thought maybe I'd get better clarity there. Well, I did! His assistant contacted him and she replied, "Angie, he wants you to sing for yourself!" *What?!* I don't do that! I'm a background vocalist! Thus, began my career as a solo gospel artist. Some refer to me as a southern gospel artist. I'm whatever you need me to be!

Lakeland, Florida

My first performance out with him as a solo artist was in Lakeland, FL, January 19, 2012. Bill Gaither is very particular about his audience. He discerns the likings of the audience by the way they sing the first congregational chorus with him. After which he then selects the song choice for each artist. You suggest and he approves. Bill cradles his audience and it's amazing to see. He knows exactly what they want. Sometimes I suggest one song and he'll say, "Trust me, kid; this audience would prefer this." I say, "Yes *sir!*" After the concert he will ask, "Did they like you at the product table?" His goal, as he always says is: "I want everyone to be a winner! We can all win!" Just as he guards the front of the stage, he guards the back. There is no foolishness of stardom, diva-ness, lateness, or nonsupport of other artists allowed. Zero tolerance for foolishness. He will laugh, joke, and play with all of us, but we know the fatherly look of discipline in his eyes and it's respected by all, and I mean *all* ages. Bill Gaither is a phenomenon in our lifetime.

Understanding my plight as a soloist, Gloria Gaither immediately mothered me for this part of my journey. Everything seemed doable with her smile of affirmation. Sometimes when the audience seemed not to understand my joy, one look at Mother Gloria, and her smile would melt away all doubt. You can see in her eyes that you have touched Heaven, as Heaven would shine through her eyes for you! Only God could have provided such a Heavenly family as the Gaither Family. Never in my singing profession days have I experienced such love from everyone involved.

But love doesn't come from everyone. I received a six-page letter from a pastor. He expressed his dislike toward my energy and commented that it would be more accepted by my own kind. He went on to say that I am treated like an animal at a circus, and when the whip is cracked, I come out roaring like a tiger. And that I should oppose such treatment and refuse to conduct myself in such a manner around white-haired, blue-eyed people with oxygen tanks.

I must say, my response was not equal to his complaint because it was only two pages. I thanked him for his letter of concern in that he thought I was out of place. I expressed to him that I understand I'm not for everyone, but with all the artists Bill Gaither has per night, surely he could find someone to enjoy. I informed him that he has about a 2-minute lay time to escape the auditorium when my name is announced, and he could return after about 10 minutes. As a rule, I sing only one or two songs at a time, so he would be safe! I loved on him and thanked him for writing, and I informed him that I was not at the wrong place. I offered him an easy fix; just leave and come back when I'm done!

I assure you that if the audience did not appreciate my gifting, Bill Gaither would not have placed me in this mold. I'm so glad for the godly insight this leader of the gospel has for all people. I'm blessed to be one of his singers!

Church of God Connections

I had a wonderful opportunity to minister with Geron Davis at a church in Chattanooga, Tennessee. The church had a contemporary feel, but when I sang the songs of old, they got with me! They love the Lord.

There was a lady in the audience who took a liking to me when I sang, "He Grew the Tree." She asked if I was available to do other ministry opportunities with her and her organization. Why, of course I was! I had no idea she was a big-time administrator for the Church of God Organization of Cleveland, Tennessee. Amazingly, she connected me with people who filled my calendar for the year! Not only had she booked my schedule with churches within the organization, she booked me in their headquarters' activities, which included the famous General Assembly. People who saw their flyer called me to ask how I was able to secure that date. I had no answer except the Lord. Not being a part of the denomination, I didn't realize how big of a deal it was. I just knew I had to be there to meet and encourage all my brothers and sisters. I walked in favor that I knew nothing of. This opportunity totally took me by surprise. From there, the dates poured in.

I had sung for Bishop Hill in the studio for years. I didn't know he was the presiding Bishop of the entire organization. He is such a humble man. When I saw his face, I felt like I was home. I knew that this was a God-ordained set up.

Since I have been introduced to the pastors of this organization by Sis. Dee Raff, I have been booked continuously and I am so grateful for her connections. To this day, I'm called by my Church of God families to come to their churches to minister. It's simply another miracle in my career life.

Booking Agents

There are many booking agents available who are great at what they do in booking artists. It is an agent's job to book you so that everyone stays in business. I truly believed this was the route for me to take, to sign with an agent. I tried it on many levels, but none worked for me.

There were those who earnestly worked to get me dates, but they can only book an artist according to a current demand. And then there were those who had no intention of booking you, but rather only to use you as a front for their venture to say they represent artists. Then there were those who had no clue how to book.

To this day, I remain open to ideas from agencies and will offer them my availability. I am always available and appreciate all help available to get my schedule booked.

Once, I signed an exclusive agreement with a promising agency. Right after I signed, communication with them became a major problem. I could not get calls answered or returned. Later, I found out they were only using me to get their roster of artists introduced to Bill Gaither. I immediately asked to be released from this agreement and they granted my request. They had no contacts and wanted me to do the calling and booking and then pay them a 20% booking fee. This didn't make sense. Why pay them and I'm doing all the work? Not! Never again exclusive. I desire to be free to do what God calls me to do, being exclusive only to Him! Again, I do have relationships around the world who graciously send dates my way whenever they can, and they *bless* me! For this, I am forever grateful!

Being a free agent has its ups and downs. One day I

received a call from a New Yorker who desired me to come and sing at his program. I was available and consented to going. Because I was traveling alone, I did ask for references, people he had worked with. He gave me several names and purchased the airline ticket.

After checking his references, I found they all seemed to be surprised at his attempt to get me there because he was in a nursing home. Upon asking him about his situation, he explained that he just wanted me to come and hang out with his family and sing. Well, I thought this to be strange and asked what his allotted budget was for a ministering guest. He explained that he never had a guest and since I was a minister, I should be willing to be his first. I explained to him that this is what I do for a living and asked what his intent was for an honorarium. He told me he had nothing and because of his desire for me to be there that God would provide. I never put a price tag on ministry opportunities, *never*! But people have to be willing to accommodate in some way, that one may survive, as I am now a full-time traveling minister. He said he understood, but all he had money for was an airline ticket and I could stay with his family. I expressed to him that if I desired to just hang out, I could do so with my own family. Thank you, but no thanks!

But then there was a ministry opportunity in Phoenix. In getting clarity, I asked the average amount of the offering that is normally given to their ministering guests. They stated that they didn't have a certain amount, but they guaranteed me that I would be taken care of. Okay, an opportunity to minister with airfare, ground transportation, hotel, food and an offering. It works for me to be able to get it done.

They were sooo much fun! They had prepared a sleigh

for me to ride on, be pulled by one man. I thought there was no way one person would be able to lift the sleigh and pull me at the same time. But he did! We had a blessed time. Leaving and once on the plane, I thought to look at the offering given me. There were about 275 people in the audience that gave me an offering of over $6,700.00! I almost passed out right there on the plane!

Always a Student

A singer will have their favorite song, and what blesses them usually blesses their audience. But this is not 100% the case. You must always be willing to learn and serve the need of your audience. This is ministry and God will lead! It can *never ever* be about your needs. If that is the case, there is no need for you to leave home. When people invite you to come, they are asking you to come and bless their congregation. People of God need to be encouraged, motivated, embraced, delivered, and healed. They don't need self-indulgence or superficial righteousness; this will do nothing and render you hopeless as a minister. You need the Lord to minister to His People! Point Blank Period!

Listen, learn, and submit to the things of God, and He will lead you to a prosperous time of ministry as well as a rewarding career. *Never compromise.* Follow the Lord at all costs. Ministry will always be a learning process. Understand God has you there for a reason and He will always let you know the needs of His people during your prayer time. You will always be a student of the Lord. You will never get ahead of Him.

It is always proper to converse with the sponsor or the leader of a people to find out what is expected and desired.

People have expectations and it is proper to serve them. You should never arrive to be served. STOP THIS ENTITLE-MENT SYNDROME! It's not pleasing to the Lord and it puts a bad taste in the mouths of the people who invited you to come. I can't begin to tell you the bad reputations ministers suffer due to bad attitudes. People have testimonies of being downright abused by "celebrity" and "wannabe celebrity" ministers. It's sad. And yes, there are sponsors and churches who mistreat their guests, but communication and paper-work, such as agreements, can help navigate around would-be bad situations. Eliminate problems on the front end as much as possible to ensure a productive time of ministry. There will be some who won't even honor the paperwork, but what would God have you do—fight them? Do you believe God would have you somewhere sprawled out on the floor fighting and cussing someone for a dollar? Or did He say, "Shake the dust off your feet and keep moving?" Isn't that what He said? You have to trust God to take care of your needs and fight your battles. Always surrender to the Lord and He will provide and order your steps to success His way!

"Starstruck-ness"

There are some people you know that cannot hold a conversation without dropping names of people they believe to be successful. I am here to tell you that these people you *sooo* admire need the Lord just like you. They desire the same thing you desire, to be and stay successful. Success has a cost. Obedience to the Lord has a price as well. Why be infatuated by someone who has no Heaven or Hell? There are people who literally bow down to celebrities and pass out because they sing a song—*really?!* Again, this is human nature, to worship the created and not the Creator. I sit back and watch because I know celebrities are only human, and backstage, they reveal just how human they are. Remember, I'm a background vocalist and I see all sorts of things backstage. These manmade celebrities are human, and they have the same insecurities and issues as the other person. Turn your worship to God who will never fail you! Understand that your promotion comes from the Lord!

I remember on one occasion, New Life had been singing to celebrities all day. It was an inauguration celebration for a president and everyone who was someone, or knew someone, was there. All day long people spoke of this person and their accomplishment, which was wonderful, but how long must one smile and say congratulations? OMG! We had arrived at 8:30 a.m. and it was now 8:00 p.m. and I was in the middle of reading the *Left Behind* series, and one of the characters, named Chloe, was about to be martyred! When they asked if we wanted to leave the premises and go to another celebrity's abode for the rest of the evening, I simply declined and asked to go to my hotel room. I wanted to read about Chloe!

Please, don't get me wrong. Networking is crucial to staying alive in the ministry. But it becomes something else when you're in a conversation that is always about one's self and one's accomplishments. Narcissism is real! And God even has a cure for that—humble yourself. You may ask "how?" Every time you hear yourself talking about yourself, simply stop and reroute the conversation. People will love you for genuine humility and appreciate the goodness of God even more. There is *no one* in this world who wants to hear about you all day, every day. *No one!* Remember this—people are people who change, but God is God who never changes. Place your hope in Him!!!

Coronavirus

As I write this book, our world is on the brinks of a deadly virus. It has been a sad time of non-touching and churching. We miss each other dearly as we are forced to stay home for everyone's safety in hopes of not spreading this virus.

As a full-time traveling evangelist, my full schedule emptied in a matter of days. No one anywhere was allowed to gather for church services or concerts. This was life-changing for me. No work! No ministry opportunities. However, there was one cancellation that came with a surprise. The pastor called me to cancel but expressed he understood what this meant to my budget. He said he felt led to bless me with an honorarium anyway. He said, "Sis. Angie, we want to pay you to stay home and be safe. This is something we will give you now to help with your budget as we know must be cancelled. But we will reschedule with you and the monies we are sending you today will not serve as a deposit for the next date. Please accept this as a gift of Love!" Glory to God, I did!

Never underestimate God and his ability to provide. Never become greater or grander than God. If He wants you to go, He will provide! God's gigs are the *best!* He pays very well and mostly inconspicuously. Sometimes there are those who have just enough budget to get you there and pay bare necessities. But then there are those who can overcompensate with no problem at all. When you are a full-time minister, it can never be about the financing from one engagement because the picture is much larger than one opportunity. God is global and so is His budget. He knows how to provide for you. You must keep walking in faith and understand that your obedience will catch up with you. And it happens all the time. Unexpected blessings flow from everywhere. Remember, He is sovereign and knows what you need and will provide.

Obedience is better than sacrifice. You can't be anointed and not obeying. He can't tell you to go and you tell Him they are not paying enough. We can *never ever* become entitled to His gift to us. We can never dictate the amount of blessing that is due us. He takes care of His own, and if your focus is mainly on finances, you will miss opportunities of God showing Himself to you and others. You will be concerned about the offering and not the move of God and why He allowed you to be there at that time. You will forget your purpose worried about a dime! Understand there will be those who will take advantage of your obedience to full-time ministry. When God shows you those people in prayer and which engagement to take and those to decline, again, be obedient. You must trust God with everything, including your livelihood.

CHAPTER 7
BACKGROUND VOCALIST OVERSEAS

I have had numerous opportunities to travel, sometimes overseas. There are no limits when you're traveling for the Lord. He owns the whole world!

NORWAY

About 30 days after being with Bill Gaither in his hometown of Anderson, IN, I received a phone call from a stranger with an accent asking if he could speak with Angela Primm. I knew the number was strange because it had too many numbers! "Yes," I responded, "this is she." He asked me if I knew of the singer Jessy Dixon. Of course I did, as I had sung on his recordings for years. He went on to tell me that he has an audience in Norway who loves him, and because Jessy is deceased, they were looking for a singer of his style to come and fill his tour dates; they asked if I'd be interested.

He had no way of knowing I had been praying and asking God for opportunities to praise, share, and spread the gospel. It's not God's will for a person to keep singing to the same people and expecting different results—that's insanity! My answer was an immediate yes. There is no need to pray about what you have already prayed for! Morten Skjaevestad, the man who called me, has been a promoter in Europe for over 30 years. He has toured more than 600 concerts with Jessy Dixon alone. He took me under his wing and has toured with Elsa Harris and I for over six years at this writing.

Meeting Elsa

Elsa Harris is a renowned, accomplished, wonderful and humble woman of God, out of Chicago, IL, who was Jessy Dixon's keyboardist. The Norwegians know her well and celebrate her like nobody's business. Oh, when you mention her name the walls echo with praise for her presence. They *love* her, and I do, too. She is one of the most precious gifts God has blessed me with while on the road. There is not a thing she cannot play! Her smile is priceless. She looks like my birth mother's identical twin if she had one.

Upon my first visit to Norway, Morten arranged that Elsa and I would meet up in Chicago to fly over to Norway together. I had no idea how she looked. I was on the phone with my niece, MiMi, as she was concerned about my traveling alone. I assured her I would be fine and that this lady, Elsa, was flying with me. At about that time, Elsa turned the corner into the sitting area where I was waiting to board the plane. Not knowing who she was, I began speaking to MiMi in hushed tones because she looked like Mommy. I said, "MiMi, God has sent Mommy to fly with me! She's looking at me and it's Mommy!" At that point, I was scared because my mother passed more than 32 years ago!

Elsa then reached over to me and said my name, "Angela?" I just about passed out. I responded, "Yes ma'am." She introduced herself to me. Lord Have Mercy! "No way you are Elsa Harris. It's impossible! You look identical to my Mommy!" God has a sense of humor. He'd set me up with a Mommy look-a-like! *Oooh, my goodness!*

Elsa has Mommy's sweet personality and disposition as well. Everything was "Yes, and what can I help you do?" Unheard of for a musician of her caliber. I was trying to help her and she was trying to help me, and Morten would get frustrated with both us for not getting it done; he'd just look at us and shake his head. Elsa and I act so much alike that she could be my birth mother.

I explained to her that I had an uncle who lived in Chicago that we were forbidden to know because he was the driver for Al Capone; for the safety of his family, he had to live in secret. He told my mother the less we knew about him, the better. The Lord would have it that before my uncle died, he was able to contact his family. When he called, he recognized my Aunt Stella's voice right away. Aunt Stella, who is my mother's sister, said he hollered to his wife while on the phone with her, "It's the baby! Honey! It's my baby sister! I know her voice! I have my baby sister on the phone."

I explained this to Elsa, who, in turn, explained to me that she was adopted and has no idea who her father's family is. She just knows that he played the piano and her grandmother, who raised her, described her hands as looking like his—large piano fingers. Elsa speaks of her father with a twinkle in her eyes. She loves him but has never met him. I'm just saying—it's possible she's my mother's niece and my cousin. She looks like us with the smile and all. God has a way that is mighty sweet!

Norwegian Choirs

We travel with Morten in his car throughout Norway. Sometimes it's a 9-hour journey—one way—that he drives (alone) from one church to the next. Upon our arrival, Morten works with unloading the car of products while we gather the choir for rehearsal for the evening's concert. You see, as we travel, we are booked at churches with choirs and singers who want to sing Black Gospel music. Morten sends them charts months prior to our arrival so they can rehearse. When we arrive, we rehearse, encourage them and run through the concert for the evening. This normally takes 2-3 hours. Then Elsa and I will have a snack and prepare for the concert that evening, most times in the pastor's study. Most of Norway's churches are historic, some being 1200 years old. Some pastors' studies look like dungeons; they would be ideal for Indiana Jones movies! But as for me, I'm asking to make sure, "Uh, *hello*—this massive door does open back up when you close it, right? That huge skeleton key *does* work? This is not prison...right?" The churches are ornate and beautiful. But remember—I don't do scary!

Morten checks on us (his girls) at least every hour, if not more. We wonder if he's resting while he's wondering if we're resting. It's the sweetest thing! And when his wife, Solveig, shows up, we are just as excited to see her! When she's on the scene, we can rest from worrying about him because she takes such good care of her husband, who is our husband on the road! LOL; confusing right? We love each other. It's a holy love. We treasure the gifts God has given us in each other.

Norway's Kolonne

We were on our way from the east to the west side of Norway during a snowstorm. We had tried three different routes, all of which were closed due to the danger of the storm. Authorities were not allowing any passage through, over, or around the mountain which separated the west from the east. Morten knew it was a day's journey, but we had a concert the next day and had to get over to the other side. We drove and drove trying to find an open passageway over the mountain. We finally arrived at the last possible option to get across. All others were closed. We had made it to the entrance when the men in yellow vests stopped the truck about two cars in front of us.

Frustrated, Morten was trying to get permission to get across before the storm started. The wind began to blow, and it was nothing like I'd ever heard before. It sounded like a mass of bears stuck in a cave. The snow began to blow and swirl, leaving absolutely no visibility. We couldn't even see the cars in front of us, but every so often we could see yellow blinking lights.

We arrived at the foot of the mountain around 4:00 p.m. They held us there until around 7:00 p.m. Thank God for the miracle of good bladders! Morten expressed he had never seen anything like this. Well, that was not comforting to hear from a native Norwegian who had traveled like this for over 30 years!

After three hours of driving in blinding snow, we saw movement. The authorities were giving instructions to all drivers. We had to travel along with other cars, inch by inch, slowly around the mountain. We had to keep moving on this way, turning what is usually a 30-minute journey across into a 4-hour one. Once across, Morten informed us that we had been part of a calculated group effort of cars and trucks that formed a Kolonne.

Norway Kolonne

We had to wait for the weight of approximately 700 cars to form this Kolonne (column driving of cars) for our safety. If we had been able to move forward alone, the wind factor would have fatally swept us into the side of the mountain. We had waited, impatiently I might add, for a plan that saved our lives! We had discussed during those hours of waiting the notion of turning around and going back to the hotel, but Morten would quiet us down with his determination, saying that we were doing the right thing by waiting to proceed forward. So, we waited. Only to find out the next day that the road we had begged Morten to retreat to was covered in an avalanche. Upon our arrival at the church the next day, a woman in the choir ran to me and hugged me and told me that it was wonderful that we pushed forward because the avalanche behind us was tragic and a man had been killed. Morten was smart not to tell us of the dangers while traveling because we would have been a couple of nervous wrecks.

Norwegian Driving

Morten drives with such ease on these snow and ice-covered roads. His calm becomes our calm. I watch him in my peripheral vision to see if he's nervous about what's approaching, and when he isn't, I try not to be. But my attempts are not always successful. At times, the only way to calm my nerves is to sleep through it. Just close my eyes and hush!

Sometimes it's just downright scary when you can no longer see where you've come from or where you're going because the roads are so quickly covered with snow. Sometimes it's just you and the side of a mountain and a drop off on the other side. Sometimes only one car can pass at a time, and that one car may be a semi-truck, and you must be patient and know to pull over. They have more round-a-bouts than they do traffic lights. They are taught to be polite and respect the roads. They are taught to be strategic in all they do. You would not survive such dangerous driving with "stateside road rage." Baby, you would die! The mentality of drivers in Norway is politeness.

Lesson learned: Rushing God can be fatal!
Wait on The Lord, He's working on your behalf!

Expired Passport

One year, while preparing to leave Nashville for Norway, I was at the kiosk trying to check in my luggage and the computer kept denying my passport, saying it was unauthorized for travel. After three attempts, I figured something had to be wrong with the machine because I'd done this over the past five years with no problem. I knew my passport was authentic and did not expire until May of that year.

I waited in line for the next attendant to explain what was wrong. She took one look at my passport and explained that when traveling overseas, you must have a valid passport with an expiration date of six months beyond your travel time. *What?!* She explained that in order for me to take this trip, I would need a passport that expired after October 1st. She also explained that the stipulation was not the airport's, but the foreign country's. I would not be allowed entrance into Norway even if I was allowed on the plane. I felt my body go numb and my eyes swell with tears. What could be done? She told me that the only thing I could do was get a new passport. She explained that there are emergency passport stations; however, none were in Nashville.

What, and where?!

My ride had left, only for me to call them back, distraught and needing to locate where to go and what to do. I googled sites for overnight passports and spoke to a gentleman who explained that it can be done; however, a person's name is normally on a list of those who have waited for a minimum of two weeks, and *then* it's an overnight procedure. I remember standing there thinking, *This is not overnight!* He then explained that the closest passport agencies that could get this done were in Atlanta, GA and Louisiana. *Still the wrong answer!*

After numerous calls to the agency in Atlanta, they explained that it was possible to get a new passport overnight; however, they were issued on a first-come-first-serve basis. There was no guarantee that I would be serviced, and the line was currently out the door, with a closing time of 3:00 pm. I told her I could be headed there right away. She explained that I needed a new passport picture and my old passport, and they would do what they could do, but there were no guarantees.

Though distraught and losing faith, I kept pushing and went to Walgreens for my photo. It is the ugliest picture in the world! My face and eyes were swollen and red from crying. I tried splashing water on my face, calming down, and thinking happy thoughts to get this picture. I forced a smile, not knowing until later that you are not even suppose to smile for passport pictures! But I did smile, doing everything I could to look as normal as possible for this photo that would have to last for years. I was stressed, not knowing whether the photo would be the only thing that would come of this overnight effort.

My niece and assistant, Valencia, offered to drive me to the agency in Atlanta, GA. At that time, I was at the mercy of any airline schedule that could get me to my destination quickly. If it happened to be in Atlanta, I would depart from there. Plus, Morten needed to rebook the flight because I had missed the one from Nashville that morning. However, I didn't know which flight to rebook. I was a mess. And to make matters worse, I realized Atlanta is on Eastern Standard Time, which meant I was losing an hour.

I decided to call my go-to for problems, Gale Mayes, my sister. She said "Angie, you can't miss anything by trying. Staying home will not get you anywhere and going will at least give you a chance! Let me call and see what I can find out." I took her advice and Valencia and I started down the highway with me crying all the way! I couldn't believe such a law was in place that I knew not of. It just seemed to me when you submit your information to the airline, someone would warn you, but they didn't. I was stuck.

Gale called back within the hour to inform me of what she had found out and it was the same that was told to me,

"You are at their mercy, no guarantees." But she encouraged me to go and told me I was doing the right thing. "Just *go*, Angie! Nothing else beats a try but a try. Go!" So I did.

We arrived at the city limits of Atlanta at 2:30 p.m. With the traffic, how in the world could we make it to the agency that the GPS said was "downtown" in a timely manner? At 2:50 p.m., we arrived at the location only to find out it was an old address. Their new location was two miles in the other direction. *NO!* I broke down again! Valencia's eyes were saddened by my mental breakdown, but she kept her calm and drove as instructed to the correct location. When we arrived, it was 3:05 p.m. and the building was closed. Not knowing where to park, we asked a gentleman outside the building if we were at the correct place for passport issuance. He said that we were. I asked Valencia to stay with the car so that I could run in in hopes that someone was still there.

When I got to the lobby, it was empty. The guard on duty explained that the place I was looking for was on the second floor, but they had stopped taking applications at 3:00 p.m., and it was too late for me to be allowed on the elevator to go up. With tears in my eyes and lips trembling, I explained my plight. She felt sorry for me and told me to do what I had to do, but she was sure the office was closed and that everyone was gone.

I got off the elevator looking for someone, anyone, *somebody* to help me. Sure enough, the sign on the glass door said "Closed." But not to me! I began to bang on the glass door. The security guard standing inside the door said, "Sorry ma'am; we are closed for the evening. You will have to return tomorrow." I explained that I didn't have tomorrow; I only had today. I begged for assistance and would not stop knocking. I needed someone in the office that could help me, and it was *not* a security guard. I prayed, *God please move on someone's heart that can help me! Please, Father! I'm desperate! Move on my behalf, Father God, MOVE! Somebody, please, help me!*

At that moment, a small-framed man peeped around the corner to see who was doing all this begging, and *why?* He approached the door and asked, "May I help you?" I explained to him what was going on and that I needed to fly out *that* day! He apologized and explained that even if he wanted to, their office was closed, and his workers had gone home, and he didn't have the authority to process and print the new passport. It was a process that required more than one person. I could see his heart softening by the look in his eyes. He said, "If you can come back tomorrow, I can give you a pass tonight for tomorrow to make sure you are one of the first in line to get a new passport. We open at 7:00 a.m. and I'll need you here by 7:30 a.m. Can you be here by this time?" *Really?!* Of course, I could! Tomorrow was better than the promise of two weeks.

He told me, "It's all I can do. It's the best I can do." He explained, "There will be a long line, but take this pass with my name on it and this will guarantee your entrance and your place in line to be one of the first." He handed me the paper through the glass doors that still had the "Closed" sign on it and told me to quit crying, calm down and not to worry; he would make something happen for me. He admitted he was a sucker for women crying! He explained if there were no issues with my passport, I should have it by 4:00 p.m. the next day and would be able to fly out that same evening. He testified that he had seen this situation happen before, but it normally took 24-48 hours to process an emergency passport after receiving a request for one; however, he would walk mine through for me personally. He said "I'll make you my priority for tomorrow. Is that okay?" All I could say was "Thank you! Thank you *sooo* much! I will be here first thing in the morning when you open at 7:00 a.m."

We were in Atlanta and I knew it was not the will of God for us to travel back to Nashville and return the next morning, considering it's a 4-hour drive *without* traffic. We had to stay in Georgia, but where and how could I afford an Atlanta hotel? Where could we stay that was convenient enough to get through Atlanta's traffic in enough time to return to the passport office by 7:00 a.m.?

With my paper in hand, I had hope, but not a solution. I got off the elevator to meet Valencia in the lobby, as the guard would not allow her entrance to the second floor because it was closed. She told me she was on her way to come get me because she knew I had no business taking as long as I did if they were closed. I thanked the merciful security guard for allowing me entrance and reported to her that they were willing to help me, but I had to come back tomorrow. I asked if she knew of a reputable hotel close by where we could spend the night because none of this was planned and I had no reservations. She says, "Ma'am, right through those double doors behind you is a hotel. This entire building is a hotel that happens to have office suites." *What?!* I was shocked; the lobby was *beautiful!* There was no way I could afford it! But like my sister said, "Nothing beats a try."

I walked through the all-glass double doors, and my first view was a stairwell made of iridescent glass that glistened and led to the dining area, which featured chandeliers and tables draped in white cloths. *White tablecloths!* I already knew:

you don't go to a restaurant with white tablecloths unless you are ready to spend some *money!* I looked beyond the stairwell to see the *marble* reception desk! *What in the world?! I prayed, Father! My nerves are shot and need a break! I've been crying since 9:00 a.m. We have been driving stressfully since 11:00 a.m. and it is now 4:00 p.m. I have begged, cried, and thrown myself on the mercy seat only to end up in a convenient hotel that only Oprah Winfrey can afford! What in the world are You doing, Father God? This is too convenient to be real and the looks of it say it isn't!*

I approached "the bench" and pleaded my case with eyes rolling in tears. The clerk felt my pain and told me the rooms are normally $350-$400 per night, but then she asked, "But what can you afford?" I told her anything around $100 would be *sooo* helpful. She said, "You got it. It will be $108, including tax. Can you afford that?" I broke down in tears to say, "Yes, yes, yes!" She then said, "Because of your troubles, I will give you a larger room. Let's see if I can find a suite for you for the night. It's only one night correct?" I answered, "Yes. We would be grateful for any double you may have. It doesn't have to be a suite. All we need are two beds, please." She said, "I have a wonderful room for you here. Allow me to take the payment and I'll issue you your keys and you can go and relax." We made the transaction and headed to the room, and *boyyyeee*, that room was magnificent! Valencia and I were in awe when we opened the door. God had gone before me and prepared the way for the passport office to be in this upscale hotel where He knew I would have to spend the night. You cannot make things like this up!

Morten found a flight for me leaving Atlanta at 6:00 p.m. I knew it was close with me having to leave the passport office after 4:00 p.m. as the office worker had stated, but it was the only flight leaving that would get me to my destination in the nick of time for a concert the following day. I knew I would have to press the issue upon my arrival in the morning.

We ate, slept, and were wide awake in the morning. After my shower, I ran to the second floor. The supervisor I met the day before greeted me like I was his aunt and he was waiting for me. Eyes rolled and heads turned as I approached the front door at 7:00 a.m., as some of them had begun lining up since 5:00 a.m. But I had paid dues the night before to be before the king in the morning! I was scared, yet I walked like Esther to that door! He spoke so loudly so that all could hear: "Angela Primm, we've been waiting for you!" I replied, "Here I am!"

My paperwork was processed immediately, and by 12:00 noon, I was notified that I would have a passport by 2:00 p.m. No way! Yes way! *(Hush, Angie, and act like you serve a God who can!)* I called to tell Valencia the news. I also called to report the news to my husband, who was disappointed by all this because he wanted me home! *(Whatever, John Primm!)* He told me he was happy for me but was hoping I'd be returning home. I explained to him that I was departing for Norway from Atlanta and would return back to Nashville. Valencia had prepared herself for the drive home alone; she made it safely to her destination and I made it safely to mine!

Needless to say, I wanted to give everyone in that passport office a gift, such as a cake or flowers or something that said, "Thank You!!!" The supervisor explained that for security reasons, they were not allowed to accept gifts in the office, but a positive review would help more than anything else

I could do. A wonderful and grateful review I wrote! They were the *best!*

"She's a Black Gospel Norwegian!"

Norwegians are sweet, quiet, reserved, but loving people. They enjoy having fun, which is how they perceive Black Gospel music—fun! To a majority of them, it's entertainment. One sweet lady was concerned that my feelings would be hurt if I didn't understand their culture of not responding to me. She wanted me to understand that they are not an emotional people and not to take their lack of response personally. She expressed to me that they loved my music but wouldn't be free to express it! I accepted her explanation gracefully and thanked her. However, I explained that they invited me to come and I was Black Gospel! I let her know that in order to enjoy herself, she would have to forget about herself and join in. And she did!

I wear Morten out sometimes with talking too much. I just forget about time restraints when I'm with my Norwegian family. I would often exceed my time allotment on stage and get in trouble! The people responded and I shared more! Getting frustrated with the idea of not being able to connect and wanting the Love of Christ to show and be experienced, I began to ask God for signs of being connected. I didn't want to just be a circus act: getting on stage, performing, and getting off. I asked God to confirm my purpose and solidify my visits in some kind of way, that I might rest in the fact that, even though my time per opportunity is limited, I'm connecting. Show me that I belong here with the short amount of time that I have to love them. I became weary in the fact that I was so far away from home for such a long period of time, and even in that time I wasn't being productive for

The Kingdom. I felt as if I were just spinning my wheels. I prayed, *"Father God, give me a sign that this is Your will. Show me that I belong, and that You purposed for me to be here, please."*

The next day, we did our concert. That evening I returned to my hotel, prepared for bed, and checked my emails. I received a message from Ancestry.com saying my results were in. *What?!* I had completed and submitted my kit for my results in January and they came in March while I was in Norway. The results were profound. I knew Africa would be there, no surprise to me. But then Ireland—ohhh. Then, with all capital letters it said "NORWAY." *What?! NORWAY?!* Father God used these results to tell me I belonged just where I was! With a new sense of purpose, I strutted to the next concert with an anointing of authority. I belonged there!!! Only God can handle details like this! Whew!!! Poor Morten, not only does he have a talking-too-much singer on his hands, but now she's Norwegian! I wish you could have seen the look on his face when I shared the news! His face said, "God help us!" *(Now she has more to talk about! LOL!)* But beyond his looks of frustration, which Elsa and I get quite often, we still see his face telling us; "I Love You!"

Singing Stories

As a background vocalist, I care about what happens behind the scenes. I love learning and reporting about the insignificant things that are not so insignificant at all—the background. I love reading about the backdrop of the Bible, the disciples, and autobiographies of lesser known people. I love the background of all things.

My performances in Norway are stories of the history of Black Gospel music. I explain that they are a part of our history. I teach that it has taken black and white people to create what is known as the Black Gospel sound. We are not Africans, nor do we sound African. We are Americans, which is the mixture of black and white together. I start singing the coded Negro spirituals that sung us to our escape. Our Black Moses, Harriett Tubman, used songs such as "Steal Away" and "Swing Low Sweet Chariot" to rouse the people and prepare for escape. Songs were cleverly used to communicate, while spoken words were forbidden. We could sing and use the rhythms of our music to keep the work of the slave unified and productive. The master had no idea, even while working, we were singing to another beat with a coded message right under his nose—escape.

The Norwegians sing the Negro Spirituals along with me, not recognizing their coded message. After we sing them, I inform them that they are blacker than they thought. LOL! We have wonderful laughs together. I then move them down the journey from slavery to our civil rights movement where Mahalia Jackson teamed with Dr. Martin Luther King, Jr. singing his favorite song written by Thomas Dorsey: "Precious Lord, Take My Hand." I take them through the streets of New Orleans, where Mahalia took the sounds and excitement of the juke-joints and migrated this music to the church with Biblical lyrics. She hated the boredom of the church and did something about it.

The Drunk Lady

Sometimes I bring the "juke-joint" to Norway. I imitate the passion of a drunk lady whose passion far exceeds the passion of a churchgoer. They love it when I play the role of "the drunk lady!" When I arrive at the venue, the first thing they ask me is, "Are you going to do the drunk lady?" I sing a song with the blues riffs that says, "My baby done left me, what am I gon'…do?" I sing it as "drunk" as possible and can barely stand up. I sing it with all the hic-cups, bulging eyes, and tears that a drunk is known for when they are sloppy. The audience falls out with laughter! Sometimes I play so drunk (and that depends on the participation of the audience) that I target a man and accuse his wife of taking him away from me! I must admit that I have fun rendering this wholesome dramatization. It's hilarious, and Elsa laughs and plays right along with me!

Then Elsa sings the blues and jazz while making the piano sing with her. It's a sight to behold and she does it sooo well with the smile of my mother. We have sooo much fun doing this, and I love the laughter it brings to the evening. From there, we journey on to the songs the choirs have rehearsed, and we minister together.

It's God's idea and we have worked together with choirs for over six years. We are excited to get there, and they are excited about us coming. Elsa and I arrive with a mind to encourage, teach, motivate, enhance, liberate, inform, and pray. We want God to have His way with each individual, with each choir. God is able to do this at every stop we make, and we allow Him to have His way.

It never fails that at the end of every concert someone is blessed and freed to worship. Some express that they have never felt such freedom in church and have never used their talent in such a way.

Each choir is different; every one of them has their own special qualities for their area. And they all do sooo well. We love showcasing them and what they've learned to their audience. You see, we know that once their audience witnesses the new, enhanced version of a choir, they will accept nothing less. It's just wonderful! Norwegians do sing Black Gospel music! We now have proof!

JAPAN

I was invited by Christ Church of Nashville, TN to take a mission trip to Japan. I jumped at the opportunity to experience Japan through song. Japanese people love Black Gospel music and we loved sharing it!

Sister Act 2

Our mission was to introduce young people, and some older people, to Jesus. We were there to share the gospel of Jesus Christ to a Buddhist nation. We traveled by bus and train to various locations filled with singers who wanted to learn more about the sound they so enjoyed.

Their depiction of gospel church was from the movie *Sister Act 2. What?!* When I would introduce myself, as best as I could, I would ask them what church they attended; they would respond, "Susta-Ac-tu." No, no, clearly, I was not communicating. I asked, "Who is your pastor? Do you have a pastor?" With the largest grin on their faces they would respond "Whoopi Go-berry!" That conversation would be over so quickly because it was evident that neither of us had any idea what the other was meaning.

To show off their chops, they would frequently sing "Jo-fa jo-fa Law we ado uh" to the tune of "Joyful, joyful, Lord, we adore You." It would be wonderful hearing them sing this song with enthusiasm and joy. They mimicked every nuance of this movie. This movie depicted how they perceived church to be in the United States, and they desired to be a part of it. The movie illustrated joy in church, and this is what they wanted! When our team showed up with joy, love and laughter, it was as if they were starving for it. *Ohhh,* the hugs we distributed during our visits were too numerous to tell!

Same Kind of Different

Speaking of hugs, I'm going to throw this in. We were waiting in line to go into a restaurant which was famous for being Steve Jobs' (founder of Apple, Inc.) favorite spot. We were excited to be there, but the lobby was too small to hold us and we had to wait outside against the building on the side-walk, which was very narrow, as are all the streets in Japan. I noticed a bus unloading people at the corner of the street, and they were walking past us to get to their destination. It was a tight squeeze for them to get past me because I was standing there in all my glory smiling and saying, "Excuse me! Sorry! You're okay."

I saw one particular lady look at me and smile as she approached me, and I returned the smile. When she got directly in front of me, she turned to face me and took both of her hands and grabbed each of my breasts and squeezed them with eyes of wonder! EXCUSE ME!!! I was in shock!!! I couldn't move because I was lodged into the side of the building with nowhere to move back or away. This lady had just *groped* me! I screamed, "Hey!!! What are you doing?!" The little lady behind her pushed her onward and returned a look of apology towards me as they continued on their journey while I stood there feeling *some kind of way*. I've never been one to fight, especially in a foreign country while witnessing love, but that right there took me a moment to settle down. Unbelievable! Daddy Gee, who I will introduce later, calmed me down by explaining that they are little people who have never experienced such proportions in their lives. It worked for a minute, but then it left me looking at him in such a way! LOL!

We stood above just about everyone. When we walked down the streets, eyes would turn and notice our difference. While they wore gloves and hats to guard them from the sun to maintain their ivory skin color, here I was parading my color, wearing no guard to keep from getting darker. They would look at me as if to say *"Whaaat?! Why are you not afraid of getting darker?"*

When we would go to universities to share, they would actively listen; however, they had their own questions. Some questions were "May I touch your hair?" Just inquisitive about our differences and no one in their past had shown allowance to approach and ask questions. Some students looked at me as if they wondered, "Does it hurt?" So sweet and freeing it was for them to get to know a different culture. And I did all I could to demolish all barriers by hugging, kissing and laughing. Whenever we left a venue, they were saying "see you later" to a new black auntie!

MiMi joined me on a journey one year and the ladies flocked to her to try their attire on her skinny, little self! They would look at me and just smile. *(Whatever!!! I didn't want to try on your tight-non-walking dress anyway!!!)* Ohhh, they'd be *sooo* happy to see her! I would just grin and bear it. *(LOL!)* Again, MiMi has always been the itty-bitty in our family, but also the loudest! The Japanese women could relate more to her size than they could mine and she was fantastic with them in sharing her freedom of worship. You had to be there to see the surprise on their faces when she opened her mouth and the huge sound came forth from this little woman. They expected it from me *(again…whatever!!!)*, but from MiMi they would buck their eyes and tilt their heads backwards and then relieve their tension with giggles. It was hilarious! I enjoyed her with them so much. MiMi loved on them and they loved her!

And when we sang Black Gospel music with them, they became free and relinquished all taught restraints. The Japanese are taught that reverence is quiet. They felt a freedom to join us where we were and do what we did. It was wonderful to watch their newfound freedom in worship. They, indeed, worshipped with us!

Non-Believers
Now the sponsor made it clear to us that just because the Japanese sang, cried and worshipped didn't make them Christian. He did not want us to be satisfied with seeing their display of emotions. His desire was for the people to become committed to the cause of Jesus Christ. He said "Sis. Angie, just because they feel the anointing of the Holy Spirit and cry during worship does not make them Christian." Wow! That was a profound moment for me. Sometimes, as ministers, we are more rewarded with the emotion we evoke than with a change of heart. We are more focused on their entertainment than we are their commitment to make change for The King-

dom. We can be satisfied with the outward tears shown and not the inward heart touched by the Lord that brings about repentance and change.

They were very honest people who would let you know they were not believers of the Gospel of Jesus. They enjoyed gospel music but were not Christian. They would state it so matter-of-factly while not being rude, but they wanted you to understand they didn't believe the same as you. They'd say, "I'm just here to enjoy you." Choir members were good to inform you of this fact. My response would always be, "It's okay to not be Christian. God does not need your approval to be God. You have me here because you enjoy something that He has created, and He is willing to share with you on this occasion. I am Christian and I want to introduce you to a God who is alive and well. A God who is full of love and laughter. Enjoy yourself today with me, as we celebrate Jesus!" They would always clap after such an exaltation.

To see them during times of worship was priceless. The presence of God would be strong in their midst every time! God knew that their disbelief was out of ignorance and not arrogance, and He honored them with His presence. The miracle of His presence is profound to those who don't know Him. Boy—after times of worship they would have more questions than an audience at a political debate! We would answer all we could and love on them as much as we could before departing for the next station of ministry opportunity. We had *sooo* many opportunities to share the love of Christ. It is true that the harvest is plentiful, but the laborers are few.

I Will Always Love You

I, along with a couple of others, were the largest (in size) in the party of missionaries. Truly, we were not prepared for the task set before us.

We were told to prepare for soundcheck and meet in the lobby of the hotel in the early afternoon to go over to the venue. The concert was hailed to be the largest event for gospel music ever in that area. They had sold over 5,000 tickets. We celebrated with them! What a success story this was about to be, until....

We all arrived at the appointed time to leave for sound check. Becky Davis and I were in the lobby waiting for transportation. The sponsor then explained that there was no mobile transportation available because the venue was within walking distance. Well, I knew I hadn't noticed a venue that could hold 5,000 people, nor one that was in walking distance. This should have been something I noticed; wouldn't you think? I graciously explained that walking is not my pastime, as one could see, and that it was 100 degrees Fahrenheit outside. But he, in return, guaranteed that it was not far enough to bother us and that we'd be there before we knew it. This was spoken by an active, skinny Japanese man! Over a mile, we treaded. After two miles, we arrived at a venue that had no seats or sitting area for the exhausted! We were there for soundcheck only! We still had to go back to the hotel to dress for the event! *Who?! What?! Where?! The devil is a liar and he's trying to kill me!!!*

I retained this information in the back of my head, and I don't even remember soundcheck. I just remember wondering, *How in the world am I going to make it back to the hotel to return again for the show and then walk back to the hotel?* I was truly overwhelmed! This flooded my thoughts! This is not what fat people do! You had to purchase this book, but this wisdom I'm giving you now is a free bonus: don't allow anyone to fool you. Whatever distance it took for you to get there will be required for your return. Don't let anyone tell you it gets shorter! It. Does. Not! OMG!!!

I died to myself that afternoon and evening. The Lord took me to Paul and the disciples and what they had to do to spread the Gospel. I was humbled because God knew I was mad! He knew I would not be effective given my present thought of killing someone for this. He knew I would have aborted the mission with my attitude. Y'all, I was one mad, plus-sized minister!

We pulled ourselves together to make it happen, Becky with her need of a knee-replacement and my need of—just a need, shoot! It was hard! But we did it and had a "come-to-Jesus" meeting afterward. Nearly eight miles in 100-degree weather was enough to kill anyone who was unprepared. Daddy Gee promised to handle it and he did!

During our time of worship, the Holy Spirit was walk-ing the aisles among the people. You could feel it! Our team was ignited with the joy of the Lord. He, indeed, honored our sacrifice. It became my time to minister a Black Gospel favorite—"Precious Lord, Take My Hand." I approached the stage and thanked them for coming and nodded to Daddy Gee to begin the piano introduction. He tried to start, but the crowd began to chant loudly, "Wit-nee U-son, Wit-nee U-son!" I didn't completely understand what they were saying, but it sounded like "Whitney Houston." I asked the sponsor standing on the side of the stage, "Are they saying Whitney Houston?" He nodded his head to say yes. The chanting got louder and I asked myself if they thought I looked like her. Do they really believe all black people look alike? Because I was standing there looking like I could be four Whitneys!

I looked to Daddy Gee and asked, "What shall I do?" He shouted over the chanting, "Sing something by Whitney Houston!" I shouted back, "I don't know anything by Whitney," and then I remembered I had sung *I Will Always Love You* at Still Waters. I struck out with this song and Geron Davis and the band fell right in sync. It was amazing! When I finished the song, there was not a dry eye in the house. I was amazed at the presence of the Lord and wondered what to do. Somebody shouted, "Do the altar appeal!" I crumbled and laughed with joy! How do you administer an altar call saying, "Come to Jesus," after you just sang a song about a woman leaving her man? But God!!! God will always use what He desires! We just have to unbox Him in our little lives and be ready for the miraculous when we open our hearts to Him!

God is always busy, and we are way too busy telling Him, "Not now God, not right now…." These people loved Whitney Houston and God knew that, and He met them right where they were. He knew what was needed to soften their hearts. The rest of the night, they heard everything that was presented with a spirit of holy excitement. God in His sovereignty had used that song to break the ice. That was a joke for the rest of that tour, when I stood there not knowing what to do with a 5,000-people-strong chant! It was *unbelievable!* That was God telling me I had control of *nothing* on His stages and that He does what He wants to do!

"Block-lee fo-u"

Y'all, I stayed hungry. All their food portions were Sam's Club's testers! I mean they all eat *small!* They just wanted us to "taste" everything and not eat nothing! Everybody was hungry! We joked about it amongst ourselves because we didn't want to offend our sponsors about their provision. When we looked up and saw a KFC in the distance, we nearly jumped off the bus! We asked (or shall I say begged) to make this an official stop. Everybody ran to the familiar restaurant and ate and then purchased chicken to go. It was *sooo* funny! Our sponsor didn't fully understand the depth of our joy but was happy to accommodate!

One evening was planned especially for our entertainment. It was an evening of thanks to us for coming. They had prepared a food buffet, special music and stage presentations, and foot massages! We were so excited to be there and enjoyed it.

Well, sitting at the dinner table right next to me was a pastor's wife. As I scooted my seat backwards to go to the buffet line, she gently held down my hand, looked into my eyes and gently said "block-lee fo-u". I smiled, not understanding what she was saying. She then held up a stalk of broccoli and repeated "block-lee fo-u." I smiled and said, "Oh, yes, broccoli. I'll be sure to get some." Trying now to leave the table, she held me down and said, "No, only block-lee fo-u." Hold on; wait-a-minute! Was this woman trying to tell me what to eat—by force? I again explained, "Yes ma'am. I will eat broccoli along with the other sandwiches, vegetables, and fruit on the buffet. May I get you something?" She said "No, thank you, I am fine. I want only block-lee fo-u." Okay! How many of you know, not only did I get up from the table, but I gathered all my belongings, for I was *not* returning to that seat! NOT RETURNING! NADA! Again—I was about to fight. LOL!

"Sing Quiet Please"

Upon our arrival in Japan, we were greeted by our host, who is a pastor. He was sooo excited to be able to introduce the various styles of worship that were represented in our group. And we were excited to be able to share! After the formal greeting, he explained that the nation of Japan is made up of quiet people, and because he had seen my videos, he asked if I would consider singing a little quieter. He explained that his desire was for the people to hear and learn and not be confused and deterred by my passion. Well, how do you sing quietly? Of course, I was there to serve, and I would try. It was the strangest task ever set before me, but I did it, and they loved it.

So, from church to church we sang "Couldn't Keep It to Myself" while we were, in fact, keeping it to ourselves! Pastor Dan of Christ Church explained that clarity was a greater need than volume. We understood and were successful in sharing the Gospel with the help of God! However, I imploded on the inside with all the joy I was witnessing as the people simply ate the Gospel like hungry little birds. Some would simply sit in one spot with clasped hands reaching toward Heaven with tears streaming down their faces. Some could hardly wait until the last song was sung to run to the stage and receive a hug.

Brother Christopher Phillip, Christ Church's Minister of Music, ministered on the keys during this tour like no one else! They ate him up! He was so humble and unassuming;

his smile is sooo inviting, which is what the people needed. People who need Jesus don't need a celebrity, star, or those of entitlement to get in the way. They need a touch from the Lord with our hands, chosen hands. Christopher has a genuine love for God's people. His gentleness toward people just shines. He also served as a mediator between the ministers (those of us on tour) and the sponsor. There was always a pending urgency from the pastor to reach the lost. Nothing was ever enough or finished.

Pastor Yasu, our Japan sponsor, loves God and the message of Jesus Christ unendingly. It is his life's calling to reach as many as he can for Jesus in his Buddhist nation. We often had just left a time of ministry to go eat for the evening, and there would be an audience there waiting upon our arrival, giving us an opportunity to minister again at the restaurant or hotel lobby! Christopher was the one to determine when enough was enough. They could have worked us all day and night. But with Bro. Christopher stating gently and yet firmly, "No, this is enough for the day," everyone understood when we were done. Ever so sweetly, Bro. Christopher led his people.

Underground Church Conference

I had sung as quietly and gently as I could the entire tour, which consisted of 18 concerts. We had some moments of outburst, for sure, but we were very careful not to lose our way and to stay focused on the mission. We arrived at the church for our final concert, and while the car windows were still rolled up, I could hear the praise songs bursting from the church. At that point, I was confused. I asked if the sound was coming from the church and our sponsor said, "Yes, Sis. Angie. We saved the best for last!" I asked if I was free to sing as loudly and freely as I would in the States and not offend. He told me yes, and that the people here would understand my praise!

I entered the doors to that church, and it frightened me! They were more Pentecostal than I'd ever been!!! They were all over the place. Some were running, some clapping, some crying, banners flying, streamers glistening, dancers parading. It was an open Heaven and I was now the one who didn't understand their praise.

I found a lady on the second row, where I was being led, and sat beside her. She was worshipping; however, I was waiting for an entrance between her sniffs to ask her what was happening. When I approached her to say, "Excuse me," she looked at me and asked if I was Sis. Angie, the one who sang "Days of Elijah." I told her I was and asked if we were still in Japan. *(I just knew we had crossed somebody's border somewhere!)* She said, "Yes, we are in Japan!" Then she asked me if I would honor them by singing "Days of Elijah" and if I would do the third verse. Well, it was a stretch for me to be able to do the two *looong* verses. I responded, "Yes ma'am, I can do the song, but there are not three verses to the song; there are only two." She told me that three verses are sung by the Japanese and she asked me to please sing it. I told her I could if she could write it in English for me, and she did! The *third* verse—WOW!

> *These are the days of Deborah,*
> *Rising and taking her place.*
> *These are the days of your servant, Esther,*
> *pleading for mercy and grace.*
> *Rise up, you daughters of Zion,*
> *The enemy we will resist.*

For we are the Deborahs of this nation,
born for a time such as this.
Behold He comes, riding on a cloud...

In awe and in tears, I folded the paper she wrote the verse on and put it in my purse for safekeeping. Then I asked her what was happening here. Why was the praise so high and free? I had not witnessed this level of praise anywhere, not even in the States! I wanted to know what was going on. There seemed to be no "church" order in their praise. What was the cause of such celebration for this gathering?

She began to explain by saying, "Sis. Angie, they probably did not explain to you where you were going for security reasons." Now, "security" is not a word you want to hear in a foreign country unless you are at the airport going home. She now had my *full attention!* Security? She continued, "You see, you are at the climax of a conference made up of underground church representatives. These people are smuggled in from all parts of the world to experience free worship once in their lifetime. Then they return to their nation to die for the gospel of Jesus Christ! Isn't that exciting Sis. Angie—you are singing to a church full of martyrs!"

Even while sitting, I felt my knees weaken and I was at a loss for words. "Exciting" was not the word I was feeling at that moment. I looked around to see all the happy faces. *Really?!* The place was bursting with joy. Then she ever so pleasantly asked me if I would close their service with their theme song. I immediately explained that I knew no songs in Japanese. I was sure I didn't know a theme song for them. She told me she was sure I knew it. Then she whispered in my ear, "When the Saints Go Marching In!"

That was it for me! I had been set up! I went totally in, with tears flying everywhere. There wasn't a Baptist sprawl, a Pentecostal jerk, or a Methodist's dignity that could express what went through my body at that moment! If I weren't so big, I would have completed a few laps myself! But I froze in my seat, in shock, realizing the task before me. When it was my time to minister, I thought I would be full of tears, but it was quite the opposite. My eyes were literally witnessing 1 Peter 4:12-13. They were rejoicing in their fiery trials. Lord Jesus! Their praise was contagious. Because they felt honorable in their suffering, there was no room for pity; praise was their rally and weapon. They had resolved to the life of a martyr and were glad in it! And I stood there asking myself, "Where is your faith in God?"

I left the service a changed person, for sure. I was honored to have had the privilege to witness such a gathering. What can one say to a people who will literally give their lives? How does God choose a person to encourage a martyr? One thing is certain—it wasn't planned by us. It was totally God, the Father, who allowed such an honor. None of us understand still yet how this event lined up. But it certainly did! Only God, who orders your steps, can know the plans He has for you!

NASSAU, BAHAMAS

I have a family in Port St. Lucie, Florida who invites me every year to their church functions. We are a close family and we love each other very much. There is nothing they do that doesn't include me!

I was there at a Women's Conference one year and the Lord, again, blessed our time together. There was a lady there who was full of the fire of the Holy Ghost. She was *sooo* anointed that you were hesitant about getting too close to her. She was powerful and you didn't approach her unless you were ready. Well, I happened to be ready and wanted all she had!

Mother Anderson was from Nassau. I told her how I longed to go there to encourage my Caribbean brothers and sisters. I explained to her that I had no contacts there and she said, "You do now Sis. Angie. You are my daughter!" All I had to do was say the word. I now travel annually to her "Big Sisters" conference held in Nassau, Bahamas!

Black Point, Exumas

Mother Anderson called me one day to inform me that she had an additional location for us to minister during our visit to Nassau. She explained it was an area that was non-commercial, and everyone lived off the water! *(You must understand that sounded scary to me!)*

When we arrived in Nassau, John and I deplaned, cleared through customs, and there was no one to be found. Unfortunately for us, elder islanders are not prone to cell phone usage, and Mother Anderson did not answer hers. I wasn't even sure if it was a cell phone I was calling. I had no clue where to go or what to do and could not get in touch with anyone. According to the schedule we discussed, we were to arrive in Nassau at 12:00 noon and leave for Black Point at 4:30 p.m. With no information on how to get to

Black Point, I decided that we needed to locate the hotel where we were scheduled to be after Black Point; I knew it was in Nassau somewhere. We simply could not remain at the airport. Distressed, I called the hotel and they were booked with no vacancies. Our reservation with them was not until Saturday and it was only Wednesday. *(Father God, help!)* Where would we stay for three nights? Surely, Mother Anderson would be searching for us by then and call me.

Pacing the lobby, John decided to walk outside again. Three minutes later, he entered the lobby with this huge grin saying, "Look who I found." I nearly passed out! I'd never been happier to see someone! She explained that she'd been looking for us outside.

At that time, we were rushing to the other airline called Flamingo Air. We were running behind and had to walk from the largest corridor, to the small one, then to the smallest to outdoors. Okay now, where were we going and where was the plane? Y'all, they walked me up to this airplane that looked like it belonged in someone's toy box in the 1800s! I looked at that plane and looked at John and I decided, "We are not going to get off the ground in this." One of the pastors' wives looked at the plane and just broke down crying before we could even get on it! The plane was so dated, but I tell you, they were the kindest and most efficient workers ever. The guy that helped us on the plane turned out to be the copilot. He had gone from loading the luggage, to loading us, to flying the plane. *What?!* Needless to say, I was completely nervous, and John was, too! He astutely looked forward and was *sooo* quiet that it tickled me! Well, it got us there on one of the smoothest rides I'd ever taken on a plane. It was simply amazing.

Upon arrival, the people greeted us with open arms. Mother Anderson began to assign villas. *What?!* No hotels? Nope. We were on the water as she had said. There were no gas stations, no convenience stores, or McDonald's. Nothing was familiar to me. They explained that there were restaurants that were only open during tourist season. My question was, "Can I just get a bag of potato chips somewhere?" There were no stores. We were assigned our own villa and our host provided us with three meals a day, including drinking water and juices. John loved it. They spoiled him rotten! He didn't have to lift a finger to do a thing. John ate fish three times a day. Fried fish, stewed fish, smothered fish. Fisheyes in, fisheyes out. Just fish! Me? I don't eat fish! My best friend became chicken.

These islanders live off tourist revenue. They refuse upgrades or commercialism to save their rural traditional island. They have swimming pigs, petting sharks, million-dollar mansions, but no potato chips. They are humble people who are so proud of their land. They are so accommodating.

We had church in the evening! They *love* the Lord! There is nothing in the world that compares to the Caribbean sound. Nothing! These people worship God and you can feel it in the air.

At our first evening service, there was a wealthy islander present who owns businesses, named Bread Boy, that transports tourists. He was so sweet! He told the people to get whatever they wanted off my product table and for me to keep a tab and he would pay it. Not ever hearing that before, I asked him to repeat what he said. And the people swamped the table. His wife, along with her daughter, reported to my villa that evening to pay me. The daughter had never heard of Louis Armstrong, whom John had impersonated that night. Her mother said she tried to explain to her who Louis Armstrong was and that he was dead. But the daughter insisted that he wasn't dead because it was John, and she had to come to the villa to hear him again! While I collected the money, John sang "What A Wonderful World" for her. We just laughed while the daughter looked on, amazed and happy!

Mother Anderson would gather the women early Thursday mornings to pray on "The Rock." It was a cleft that stuck out in the ocean that you could walk on to view the water. It is simply breathtaking! But remember, I'm not an outside person, so me—I'm looking for snakes! But when we began to pray, all my fears were gone! Mother took her girls and prayed over us like nobody's business. Her aggressive praying on this rock became a serious concern for her and us. We quickly became armorbearers for one another as she targeted each of us as the Spirit led. I could barely see for crying! The Spirit of the Lord was mighty on that rock and Mother meant business. She knelt, stood, laid, paced, circled, and declared in prayer over her girls. I had never witnessed anything like this before. She kept pushing my belly like she was mad at it! She kept praying loudly "FIRE!!!" I was no good! No good at all was I. But I couldn't stay in that place because I had to be alert for the next person to keep her from falling off the rock. Mother was a midwife and she delivered on this rock! Pastor Sheila approached me after prayer and said, "Sis. Angie! There is a book in there! Write it! Write it, Sis. Angie! Write! God is saying Write!" Again, I was no good!

At our last session for the afternoon, they fed us. They announced the menu for the afternoon was pig feet, fish or chicken. Of course, my choice was my friend, chicken. They brought John some fish in a bowl, laying in some sauce that he said was good. Okay. Pig feet came and some said that was good. When my chicken came, white in color in a lemon sauce, I felt sick. *What could they have done to that chicken*, I wondered. I didn't want to hurt the hosts' feelings, but I knew I couldn't swallow something that made me feel queasy by simply looking at it. I could see the bumps in the skin of the chicken. Everyone ate like it was wonderful. I'm just not a culturally educated diner. If it doesn't look like Momma's, I'm not adventurous enough to try it. I'm just not. I'm sorry! This is why I know I'm not called to be a missionary. I just couldn't do it!

They understood and were *sooo* kind about it. I had picked at the chicken to find meat, but there was little to be found on the wing that was swimming in this sauce. So, I politely asked if there was a place in one of these tourist restaurants that had fried chicken. One of the hosts said, "My cousin owns a restaurant that is not open at the time, but I can ask if they can fry chicken for you." I asked them to please do so; I was so hungry! Then everyone else chimed in! "Me too!" Ah-uh, everybody else was hungry for fried chicken too! It was *wonderful!* Again, they catered to Johnny-boy (John) and fixed him a wonderful special drink that had gingerroot in it. He asked for that drink for the rest of the tour—just spoiled!

God blessed our time together and we hated to leave! The services were power-packed and the people were loved and gave love. As of the writing of this book, we have made two visits to Black Point! It is God's Country. Bahamas is Paradise.

JERUSALEM!

There has never been a location I have desired to visit more. I have read about it, sung about it, prayed about it, and imagined it all my life. The opportunity arrived where I could visit and sing! Unbelievable! I had first visited in 1994 with my church family; however, it was not a singing gig for me. But the next visit was!

Israel 2020 Journey of Pentecost

Networking is everything when it comes to ministry. The life you live will be the life that leads you to awesome opportunities.

Having been to Jerusalem before, I wanted to make sure my next visit was thorough, well organized, and covered in wisdom. There is so much to be seen in this land and I wanted to be able to take full advantage of my time there with tour guides who were well-versed in the Scripture and knowledge of the land.

I have an incredible relationship with the Church of God organization out of Cleveland, TN. When I read in a flyer that they were planning a trip there, I wanted to go! Whatever the cost, I wanted to go! I knew it would be so well-organized that not a minute would be wasted. How could I afford this trip on my budget? I needed a miracle from Father God for this expensive trip—and there was God!

I reached out to my sister who works at The Church of God headquarters and asked if a singer was needed. She explained to me that the schedule for Israel had been set already, but she would check on things for me. I explained that

I didn't need to be compensated; I just needed to be there!

She contacted Bishop Hill for me and he made "otherwise" arrangements for me to be able to go. You ask what I mean by "otherwise?" The budget for Israel was spent, but if I was willing to pay and go, they would definitely use me while I was there. I consented! Anything for Jerusalem! He started out by discounting the trip for me, then he began to book me for dates to help me pay for the trip. Yes, Bishop Hill did this for me!

I was short $1,500 and the final payment was due December 3, 2019, and it was November. Yikes! My sister in Texas had made reservations to go with me and decided she couldn't do the walking. Instead of her getting her refund, she gave me her $800.00 deposit to go toward my trip. *What?!* God kept smiling on me and causing me to trust Him all the way, and I did! I rode the finest of tour busses, had the most knowledgeable Holy-Ghost-filled tour guides, stayed in 5-star hotels, ate at the most exquisite restaurants, and sang at every stop to the glory of God. I was able to express, through singing, my gratitude for everything He had made possible for us to experience in His Holy City, Jerusalem.

There is not a feeling on earth that compares to the one of seeing Jerusalem upon exiting the tunnel and entering into the city. No words! The Holy Ghost simply yanks your spirit up into ecstasy! *Ohhh,* we cried, laughed, leaped, hugged, and screamed as we entered, while Tisha (our assigned tour guide) played the song, "Jerusalem," over the bus' loudspeaker. Yes, it was Heaven on earth, and we could not wait to walk the streets of Jerusalem!

We arrived on March 1st and I was ready to begin

singing February 29th. My heart raced for the opportunity to bless and be blessed with this gift God has given me. What did God have in store for this trip? What would I see? Who would I meet? What would be happening during my stay? What songs would be appropriate for such a profound place? Every scripture you've ever read comes to life in Jerusalem.

Being bashful, *(Don't judge me! I am bashful! LOL!)* I always want to make sure I'm in a space of welcome and not of intrusion. Bishop told me to tell him when and if the Lord placed a song on my heart and he'd allow me to minister it. Are you kidding me?! I told him he would be better off by telling me when *not* to sing. I heard music in my spirit when I got off the airplane in Tel Aviv. I was sooo ready that I needed to be calmed down!

Sea of Galilee

My first opportunity to sing in the Holy Land came in the middle of the Sea of Galilee. We rocked the boat, baby! LOL! The Arabic boat staff was a bit surprised at our fervor, as well as some in our group, as we began to rejoice and dance to the song "This is the Day!" We clapped and danced as if on land with no fear of tipping the boat! I was raptured in the thought of knowing all that God had demonstrated on this water and rendered exuberant praise for His sovereignty and goodness. You could see the workers join our praise with their hand clapping and foot stomping, even though in shock! When I "returned to earth" to finish the song, I noticed several people holding on to the rails of the boat in fear! God met us in the middle of the sea on that fisherman's boat! Hallelujah!!!

Spring of Harod (Gideon's Fountain)

Every location in Jerusalem is special. There is a holy reverence that follows you everywhere you go. There's an anointing in the air that simply consumes your being.

Next we approached Gideon's spring, the pool where God instructed Gideon to downsize his army and choose only 300 men to fight. It was at this site that Gideon had to trust and obey God for the winning of his battle against the Midianites. We were told to take pictures, but to consume the water at our own risk because it was extremely potent with vitamins that could cause the need for frequent toilet stops. But pictures we did take.

Bishop made a short talk to bring the site into focus and asked if there was a song on my heart. I responded that if Gideon had been a black man, he would have struck out singing "I Will Trust in the Lord Until I Die." The Holy Ghost energized our harmonized choruses, and people began to gather to find the sound of this Black Gospel music. They swayed, clapped, joined in with their foreign tongues and we had CHURCH! No instruments, no choir, no building— only this holy spring at our feet and the open Holy Heavens above our heads. We declared with our voices and hearts that we would trust in the Lord! A moment I will never forget! I could have stayed there and led worship with tourists all day! They were curious about our sound. One Spanish gentleman hollered from the other side of the spring, "Memphis! I love it!" We laughed and kept sharing the sound.

Voice of Hope Radio Station

We had the privilege of touring Galilee's 24-hour Gospel radio station. The people there work so hard around the clock to ensure that the message of the returning Messiah is broadcast throughout their land and the surrounding non-Jewish areas. Everyone from miles away can tune in to hear the gospel of Jesus Christ.

While setting up for a time of ministry in song outside on a prepared stage, I was told that an Israeli broadcaster was in a room adjacent to the touring room, and he was watching and rocking to the Gaither video, "Said I Wasn't Gonna Tell Nobody." Bishop Hill explained to him that the singer of that song had just toured the place and was outside in the stage area. He couldn't believe it because he had seen all the visitors pass by and I was not one of them! *(Make-up does miracles for this girl! LOL!)* Convinced, but still not sure, he ran outside to find me. I saw him running toward me and the only thing I could do was brace myself and embrace him as he rushed me, and then watch him pull away to determine if I was really me! LOL! We laughed and it was so special singing to him and his audience, as I sang, "Yes God is Real." He'd called his people to tell them I was there, and the courts began to fill up as they heard the sound of Black Gospel music. You could tell it was a culture shock, for some looked astonished as I delivered God's message in song with joy, passion, and dance.

Beautiful "demonic" Music

We had left the pit that is said to be where Jesus was placed after His trial, while awaiting His crucifixion. We descended into the pit singing "Oh the Blood of Jesus" and ascended singing "I Know It Was the Blood." What a powerful and moving time of ministry that was. With my voice being so loud, even while singing quietly, people from everywhere joined in our song. A sweet, yet solemn, time of worship it was.

When we reached the courts just beyond the pit where it is said that Peter denied Christ, we heard a beautiful sound of song ringing over our heads. It was Arabic music being piped through the atmosphere. When I began to hum along, the tour guided explained to me that it wasn't wise because I was joining in on an abominable and pagan chorus. I was shocked! Why, it sounded *sooo* beautiful! He went on to explain that the Arabic people understand the power of music and every day they bombard the atmosphere with their message to oppress its listeners and keep control. WOW! The power of music. They then instructed us to SING! We began to sing "The Blood Will Never Lose Its Power" until the pagan music stopped. We cleared the air with songs about The Blood! Hallelujah!!!

The Tomb

Leaving there, we went to the Tomb. Allow me to tell you right here—He is not there! Glory to God! Hallelujah!!!

Again, the mood was solemn, and the anointing was very, very heavy. Crying, amazed, weighted with His glory, and with much gratitude, we took communion. I began to sing traditional communion songs that were not familiar to our "listening" audience. People gathered to enjoy and join in our song.

One Israeli lady standing to my right looked so puzzled and lonely. I heard the Holy Spirit tell me to embrace her. I asked Him if He was sure because a large black woman singing loudly could frighten anyone who is not familiar with our church customs. But while singing, "Because He Lives," I heard the Lord say, "Hug her now!" I began to approach her while saying, "Father, if she takes off running, don't blame me for scaring her! This is Your doing!" To my surprise she lifted her arms and fell into my bosom and cried like a baby as I cradled her!! I felt the Lord lifting burdens during our embrace and no words were spoken. Love filled that encounter and she wouldn't let go! At that point, I became nervous because we had been informed that Christian proselytization was against the law and one would be prosecuted to the fullest extent of the law. But as God would have it, LOVE knew no boundaries and it could not be judged or prosecuted. All I did was hug and sing!

St. Anne's Church

We traveled to St. Anne's Church, which is the site reverenced for being the location of the home of Mary's mother. They have built a sanctuary famous for its acoustics. As beautiful as it was, we were instructed that we had only a few minutes there because others were waiting in line to enter the small space.

As we took our seats, the Lord spoke to me, telling me to just sing! In awe, waiting for Bishop to finish speaking, he gave the mic to Minister Jonathan Swayer who sang and then handed the mic to me. The only song that would exit my lips was "Just as I Am." Before I knew it, I was being helped out of the sanctuary while the next group was picking up the song where we had left off. Hearing them sing, I quickly returned to the sanctuary and became a member of their group. I could not stop the singing and didn't want to exit His presence in that sanctuary! This was *sooo* life-changing to me. A simple acapella song from the heart does the Lord good. Whew! I'll never forget the feeling I had as He smiled upon our worship in that sanctuary.

Miracle Uber

From the exuberant entrance to this Land to our sad exodus, God made a way for His people to experience all that He's done and is going to do with His Holy City, Jerusalem. Everything today points in that direction. It's the most sought-after land in the world, yet mysteriously protected and provided for by our awesome God.

God prepared a way for my travels there and I needed a way made for my travels to return home. Our day to return home was March 10, 2020. Corona had hit the land and everything as we knew it was shutting down. My husband had started calling me two days prior to us traveling home, worried about me being quarantined in Jerusalem or in New York, which is where my layover was. He was nervous, as was I! I knew with all the flights cancelling, we needed to get on a plane returning to the States, and I needed to return home to Nashville. If I had been quarantined anywhere besides home, I knew that John would be okay, but I had a puppy who needed her Mommy! Lord, get me home! LOL!

For the journey to Jerusalem, I had flown Southwest Airlines to get to New York. However, I had to travel from New York to New Jersey to meet up with the church group so we could travel to Israel together. The return trip required me to travel from New Jersey back to New York from where I would fly home. Unfortunately, Southwest no longer operates out of Newark, NJ, but that didn't seem to be a problem, considering a frequent shuttle travels between the two airports. However, while trying to make my shuttle reservation, I discovered their schedule would only allow for my transport from NY to NJ and not NJ to NY. Besides, the shuttle didn't begin service until 11:00 am, and my flight departed much earlier than that. How was I supposed to get to New

York?! To take an Uber there would cost more than my flight at $166 one way!

Leaving on the last flight out of Israel (because of the Corona virus), we landed in Newark, NJ at 4:00 a.m. Preparing my heart to book an Uber at the price the app had quoted me prior to leaving Israel ($166), I briefly checked my emails because I had been in the air overnight. And there it was! An Uber coupon made available to me, lying in my emails. I clicked on the link, knowing any discount would help with this rate. Choosing the most economical car available, I booked it. After applying this coupon, the rate of $166 dwindled down to *$46.27! WHAT?!*

I ran through the airport trying to get to the car before the app changed its mind! I sped through the border with global entry, picked up my luggage, and looked for a scooter. (I knew it had to be only a scooter for $47!) A taxicab driver approached me explaining he could beat any price to transport me to where I needed to go. I asked him if he could beat $47 and he looked at me in amazement and asked if I booked a bicycle. I told him I didn't care what it was so long as it got me to LaGuardia Airport.

While standing on the curb looking for my "scooter," a huge brand-new white Ford Excursion approached the curb. I moved out the way so that I wouldn't miss my ride. The driver exited the car and asked me if I was Angela. I asked him if he was James (according to the app's information) and immediately tried to locate the car's license plate number. And there it was! The only car available that time of morning and God sent it just for me! All the toll lines were short— which surprised the driver—and we made it there in record time. ONLY GOD will set you up in order to show out! It was

His final way of telling me that He has wanted me to take this trip to Israel, so He made a way—even down to the UBER!

CHAPTER 8
BACKGROUND VOCALIST ON THE BIG SCREEN – THE MOVIES

There have been movie opportunities to be in choirs throughout my career. You are often used as fillers or choir members and it's fun to do. However, one experience led me to Hollywood, CA.

The Death of a Nation
I received a phone call from the writer and director of the movie, *The Death of a Nation*, who'd seen the video of me with Jason Crabb singing "Precious Lord, Take My Hand." He said he enjoyed the video so much that he went to my website to investigate who I was. Once he saw the songs I sang, he wanted to know if I would sing "The Battle Hymn of the Republic" and "Precious Lord, Take My Hand" in his movie. Thinking that it was all a hoax I said, "Sure."

I called my sister, Gale and we laughed about it. I told her if he called back, I'd discuss a check and that would surely end all conversations. This was in October 2017. Well,

I didn't hear a thing from anyone and had forgotten all about it. Come January, I received a call from his producer. *What?! Is this real or Memorex?* Now I'm about to be annoyed because whoever this is is wasting my time! He asked if I would be available to tape the scene in the movie in March. I told him I was not available in March because that's the month I would be in Norway. He quickly responded and told me they would schedule the taping around my schedule because the writer really desired to use me. I'm like, *"Okay, whatever."*

However, both the writer and producer were *sooo* sweet to me and called to discuss immediate availabilities. I was beginning to believe something was in the making but I just didn't know what! They were so hesitant because this was a political movie. I told them I had no problem singing for anyone. My gifting is not my own and I will use it for whomever God allows. I am not a political singer. If you want me and it's lyrically correct, I'm available! I don't show up in anyone's studio asking if they are democrat or republican before I sing. That's nonsense! I'm a session singer and hired to sing, not campaign. They wanted to know if I was signed to a label. I told them no. Then they asked if I was a union singer and how much I would charge. I explained that I was not in the union and understood if that was a problem and they could not use me. They explained they were independent and did not need me to be in the union, that they could use whomever they desired. *(What?! I was told without being a union member I would never be on the big screen…but okay, if you can do it! I'm still peeping with my big eye!)*

They asked if I knew a black church choir with choir robes who would be willing to sing in the movie with me. I told them I was sure to find the choir, but the robes would be a problem. Then they asked if I knew of a church with stained glass windows and pews. Now that was a tall order that I could not help them with.

They loved the track for "The Battle Hymn of the Republic," but they thought it was too celebratory for its placement in the movie. The producer asked if I would have a problem with his music director going to Prague and using their orchestra for a more traditional arrangement. Well, heck no, I didn't mind! Mommy's song with an orchestra. I didn't mind at all! This was wonderful...if it was real. I still didn't know these people. Who would have the time to play on my phone like this?!

They asked if I would be available to tape the beginning of February. I said yes! They hired a Hollywood producer who called me to discuss the key and arrangement. He, in turn, laid a piano track and created charts and sent it to Prague for their rehearsal. He then flew there to orchestrate the laying of the track with all the instrumentation. He consistently kept me in the loop, which was so exciting, hearing all the particulars of the process. It is said to be cheaper to fly to Prague and use their musicians than it would be to use union musicians in the States, and I have heard of many producers who travel to Prague for orchestrations. I didn't know who these people were, but they sure did have a good game if it was a hoax. But I didn't mind; I was all in because I wasn't losing a thing but time. So, if it works, it works! I was waiting around every corner for them to ask me for a dollar, and that wasn't going to happen. So, let them pursue—on their dollar.

Then they asked if I had a studio available to lay vocals. Of course, I did! Within the week, we were in the studio laying lead and BVGs. At this point, I'm still in shock, yet skeptical. I explained to every singer that I did not know these people and that they promised to have a check ready at the end of the session for studio work and a separate check for the movie taping. Everyone was excited and trusted me. I was nervous as a cat in a room full of rocking chairs! Trè Corley, my white son, dropped in their music tracks via internet and loaded it in his computer. When he opened the files, the track was massive! The sound took your breath away; it was overwhelming! I couldn't believe it and all I could do was cry. Mommy's favorite song with a Prague orchestra! Then it was time to add the vocals. We recorded BGVs first, and at the end of the session, everyone was paid for the day. They had overnighted everyone's check! Well, sir! I returned the next day to lay my lead vocal, and during the time in the studio, I received my check. This is how Hollywood worked for us. Everything completed within two weeks. The Prague trip and all!

Scarritt Bennett Center

So far so good, everything they promised, they did! The staff of this production was supernaturally kind. They made me wonder after each call—what is really going on? I was falling in love with each and every person I came in contact with! It was now time for the taping. They explained that the cameras and cameramen were flying in from Los Angeles the day before to prepare for the taping. I was curious and asked if all this prepping and taping was for the two songs or were there other scenes being shot here in Nashville. They said it was just the two songs. They explained that they had found the perfect place in Nashville *and* they had found choir robes. *What?!* The choir robes were blue, but they said I could wear any color as long as it looked nice. Of course, I wanted to look like the choir as much as possible; I am a background vocalist with front-line opportunities.

I ventured out to find the address given me, looking for a small church with stained glass. I found the parking lot, but there was no small church in sight. I decided I needed to get out and find it. Gale and I arrived around the same time. While walking toward a building, she noted a lighting machine propped against a building with stained glass. I'm asking myself, *Is this it?* It couldn't be. It was a massive and magnificent edifice. Gale said "It has to be the building. That machine is a lighting machine used in movies to create sunlight, and they are shining it through the church's windows. Angie, this is the real thing!" She could sense my hesitation, my uncertainty. All I could think about was the possibility of having all these choir members take off from work and not be paid.

It was a wonderful experience. I walked that aisle for the one song from 11:00 a.m. until 4:00 p.m. They finally said they had enough shots to use for editing. They were happy and so were we. And everyone received a check at the end of the taping!

The Red Carpet Event

Thinking everything was done and over in February, I received a call in June asking if I could go to Hollywood for the movie's premier during the first week of July? Excitedly, I looked at my calendar only to discover I was booked. *Ohhh nooo!* I had to be at the General Assembly Conference for The Church of God on that Wednesday.

They explained that the premier event was Tuesday evening. They expressed that they really wanted me to be there and they would do anything to make this happen. But I explained I couldn't because I had to be on stage in

Orlando, FL by 9:00 a.m. Wednesday morning. There was no way we could do that. The producer said, "Where there's a will, there's a way." He asked if I would be willing to take a red-eye flight from California to Florida that would get me there in time to get on stage Wednesday morning. Because I would have to leave so suddenly Tuesday night, they asked if I would be willing to come Monday, the day before, to meet producers and do a radio interview. I told him I would *love* to! He kept me on the phone while he booked a first-class sleeper seat for me. For me?! He said if I was willing to make this sacrifice for them, they would do this for me. I didn't even ask him to do this; he just did it!

The arrangements were simply wonderful and humbling. They had a limousine awaiting my arrival in Los Angeles. The hotel was divine and within walking distance to the opening theatre. I met wonderful people on Monday night. They had scheduled a movie viewing for a select few with a question and answer panel afterward. Because I was leaving early Tuesday evening, I was permitted to attend. My mouth was open the entire time and when the last scene was shown with me and the choir, I was in awe that God could and would and did do something this marvelous! *Only God!*

Numb, I walked back to my hotel room while understanding that God had arranged all of this for me, a background vocalist. I was treated royally. They called me every hour on the hour to ensure that I was alright and that I wanted for nothing! That was Monday night. Tuesday arrived and I had to dress for the evening's gala, The Red Carpet Event. What did I choose to wear? What else does a background vocalist wear? Black! It was a high-low dress with a train. I wore pumps with rhinestones and pearls with an updo hairstyle. I felt wonderful and ladylike during my preparations. It was fun until it became nerve-wracking! Questions began to fly around in my head: How should I walk? What do I say? Did I need an escort? What all am I supposed to do? This was *sooo* out of my element! I don't do celebrities; I have always run in the opposite direction.

I left the hotel room and a car was waiting to take me around the corner that I had walked around the previous night. *Really?* Upon my arrival, they announced who I was and escorted me to the front of a line that was wrapped around the building. Reporters began to question who I was, and at that point, I didn't even know who I was! You're instructed to wait your turn to walk in order not to clog the walkway. The cameras took their shots, then a brief interview regarding my role in the movie at the end of the runway, and then up to the reception prepared for special guests before the movie began. I still didn't know these people, but by then, they had begun to "be real" to me, and I loved being with them! People this gracious had to be a Godsend.

During the reception, I walked, greeted and ate hors d'oeuvres. I was able to put faces to the voices I had grown to love! They kept expressing how much they loved the last scene. They expressed how it was truly a defining moment in the movie. I hated that I couldn't stay for that evening's showing because I had a plane to catch. This event was God truly kidnapping my schedule and making it His own. I saw the Lord "close up and personal" all throughout this entire opportunity.

CHAPTER 9
BACKGROUND VOCALIST'S PERSERVERANCE

How does one understand the path God has prepared for them? How do we know when an opportunity is a God-thing versus a distraction?

Understand, the enemy knows your potential. His best work is in the field of arts. This was his position in Heaven. Lucifer was an artist. He went from worshipping God to worshipping himself. Does this sound familiar? You will see it all the time with stage personalities; a perfor-mance suddenly, ever-so-slightly, becomes all about them-selves. Run from such people! This attitude is contagious. It spreads rapidly. When you begin to believe you are more deserving, better than, and entitled to, you are on your way down, just as satan fell—down. The symptoms are as old as the Heavens. Recognize them and discard them immedi-ately. It is imperative to stay humble. People will set you up for failure, especially when you give them the tools to do it with—your pride.

Pride is a demonic setup designed by Lucifer himself. When a conversation amongst people is all about you, be careful. "Me," and "It's all about me" is a familiar seed of satan. Self-indulgence is his specialty. Some call it "diva behavior" and others call it "grandiosity." Either way, it's self-indulgence that has tentacles from its maker, satan.

How do you last out here in the session world? The answer is God! Even when people are not calling you for session work, God still has a plan. You have to trust God everyday of your life. He is your source. No producer, artist, or gig in the world can out-pay God! You must understand that your talent is not who you are. Your talent is only a tool used to fulfill your purpose. When opportunities change, change with them.

Here is a quote by the late Pastor Danny Chambers that changed my life and I often use it to help others: "In times of change, the learning inherits the earth, while the learned find themselves beautifully equipped to handle a world that no longer exists." We must follow His cloud by day and His fire by night. How do you see His cloud and fire you ask? Through prayer and staying close to Him. Always find time to seek Him. He is to be your compass.

When it doesn't feel right, 90% of the time, it isn't. Sometimes you will miss the leading, but God has a way of herding His sheep to still waters. He knows what you need. If we could only believe this, we would be a lot further along in our journey. He wouldn't have to keep coming to find us as we are drawn to rushing waters that can drown us. He says, "No My child, I desire you to come this way to the quiet and still waters. Trust Me. I know all that you need. My plan is hidden in you.

"Trust Me to reveal it in due time."

Many times through the years, I have wondered, "Lord, why didn't they call me for the gig?" This is a common question among session singers who are always looking to be employed. If you're not careful, satan will have you anxiously living for a call from someone, at all times, for your livelihood. This is where things get ugly, mean, and conniving. You slip into the "crabs in a bucket" syndrome. You'll cheat and lie to be behind the mic to make $100! Lord, Jesus save us!

I've had session accounts for years that were stolen by other singers who'd arrive early to tell producers what I couldn't do and how they could do a better job. Next thing you know, the client is calling them for a session as the newly appointed session leader, a role that I had been previously hired for. I'd walk away wondering, "When and how did they become the session leader over a session I have led for years?" The client would bend a listening ear to lies informing them of what I could or could not do, supposedly as "my concerned friends." Then for the sake of the client loving me, they'd believe them and relieve me of the stress they were told I was under, which is also known as stealing gigs!

But in this business, you have to know that God has a way and what's for you is for you. There is no lie from hell that can keep God from fulfilling His purpose in you. I'm talking about leading you beside still waters. I'm talking about Him preparing a table before you in the presence of your enemies. I'm talking about God's divine plan and the tools He uses to carve you into His masterpiece. I'm talking about a God who misses nothing!!! There is nothing that takes Him by surprise, and on this fact you must rely. He is God and your provider. You will find yourself removed from the situation altogether, only to be positioned at another station! *Glory to God!* You will find yourself drinking from fresher water, as the dust of their jealousy, thievery, and pride has muddied the other! Follow God; He will lead you!

God begins His transformation of me right before my eyes. Watch this! I'm writing about God and His sovereignty. I'm writing to encourage you to rest in His plan for your life! God has a way of shifting things in your favor. He shifts for those who love Him and render their lives for His purpose. For those who have a heart for His Kingdom, He will navigate for you, always. Just listen and move! *(Now watch this...I don' got happy over here! LOL! Oooo-Weeee, Hallelujah!)*

CHAPTER 10

BACKGROUND VOCALIST'S ENDURANCE
(MULTIPLE STREAMS OF INCOME)

I have always worked for a living. All through high school, I worked as soon as someone would hire me! Starting at Marshall's department store then to Indiana National Bank at age 15.

My mother, who was married to my alcoholic father, had to provide for her family with numerous streams of income. She worked as a senior citizens' director at a community center 10 hours a day, sold Amway, Avon, Stanley products, and her crafts. She was a workaholic. If it sold, she wanted to sell it for her family. She worked excessively to cover the lack of my father's ability to provide. He was a functional alcoholic who worked every day to be able to get a drink.

My father worked at a renowned country club that allowed him easy access to daily alcohol. After a two-week period of his working, I glanced at his paystub and noted it stated $18.00! They allowed him to do the work he could, only to run up his tab and deduct it from his pay. It was a win-win for them, but a great loss for my mother. She was left with nothing to take care of the household. The burden of provision was all on her shoulders. With this being her plight, she taught all her children to work and take care of business. Waiting around for a handout and laziness was not an option. Work!

Never Put All Your Eggs in One Basket

Never believe that because you are talented someone owes you a check. No sir! You are only paid for your talent as long as it's needed. The world has a way of moving on without you. Albertina Walker had a saying that is true: "Out of sight, out of mind." People are born "flippers." People go for what they need at the moment. It's not disloyalty; it's life. It's how people live. That doesn't make it right; however, it's the ruling of society for survival. Things move on and you must move on and learn to hear God as He dictates and makes a way for you and your purpose.

Your purpose doesn't always look like your desire. If you are focused on your desires, you will be disappointed. Because what worked then doesn't work now. Everything must change. This is where the Scripture comes into play, Psalm 37:4 (NKJV) "Delight yourself in the Lord and HE will give you the desires of your heart." God will stick by you through the ages and changes, knowing what is best for you! *(Good God from Zion!!! I can shout right here!!!)*

With that being said, one stream of income was not acceptable or adequate. I have always desired to work! Having all my eggs in one basket was not acceptable for me. Always have a plan "B." Some would call this "faithless;" I call it doing the best you can with what you have. I call it being on the lookout for what God is doing and being ready and able to move with the cloud and fire anointing. It's being engaged and not waiting for a phone call to affirm your calling, but being found doing until He returns.

There is a saying amongst session workers that we seem to have, "Feast or Famine." This means that one day you can be called to do ten songs, and then not be called for the next month. I knew this probability and always sought employment to supplement any lack.

I was the administrator for Bobby Jones for four years. But working during the day and singing at night for him was not a comfortable position for me. It was too many "eggs in one basket." I began to seek other employment while yet being a background vocalist for Bobby Jones Gospel.

Upon seeking out other sources of income, a job became available to me in the industry. I became the radio promotion's director for a Black Gospel record label in Nashville, TN. Seeing so much misconduct backstage, I ran to the church for employment! I left the label and became employed by Born Again Church—my church! Be mindful, I was still doing sessions and on the road during weekends with New Life.

Still singing whenever I could, Born Again Church's schedule of events did not allow the flexibility I needed to do sessions and travel. After 14 years at my church, I began to seek employment elsewhere because I knew I was called to sing, as well as live, and I needed other incomes to support my life and my gift to sing. All the while, God was directing my path and ordering my steps to fulfill His purpose in my life.

Now listen to me; I don't make light of the fact that goodbyes are hard and transitions difficult. But changes are necessary in taking you to the next level of living, learning, and thriving. This is where you "blindfoldedly" trust God. When doors begin to shut, look for the open window! It's there! As long as you have the Lord, there is hope! He must be the chief administrator of your life. He has and is orchestrating the plan for your life. See God in all things and listen to His voice. Thank Him for all revelations given to you. Once He sees your gratitude He will begin to reveal more to you!

Please, indulge me for another minute. Some may be asking, "Where is your husband, John? Why am I needing to work when I have a husband?" *Listen Linda, listen!* As long as I am able to work, I will. I never believed in musicians sitting at home and laying the burden of life on one person. If you can work, *do it!* Some people are gifted and believe it's against God's will for them to have a job. God forbid such foolishness! If your gifting is not able to pay your expenses for living, then your gifting is not your living. Neither are you supposed to impose your living on someone else so that you can sit on your behind and wait for a call to come for you to sing to make $100 and then go home and sit and wait for the next call. No ma'am! No sir! Work until the day is done! Make yourself useful to your family and to yourself. There is nothing like having a purpose-filled day. If you're staying home to write a song, make sure your writing days are covered so that your withdrawal to write doesn't take away from your family. Work! This is my motto and the motto of our ancestors.

There were some session singers who would not call me for work because they said I didn't solely depend on sessions for a living and didn't need the work because I had a job. Firstly, you can't judge what someone needs for their expenses, and secondly, your not calling me is only one stream stopped by you, and not by the Lord. God knew I wanted to do what was best for my family, and He provided continually, with or without their calls.

Session work can really become cliquish if you fall into a certain mode of thinking. If you believe it's about you, then it's only you and your singing partners that can get the job done. People have their choice of who they want and don't want to sing with, as I have mine, based on those who get things done. But there is a way to choose people and not hurt others. There is enough work available for everybody. You do your part and I'll do mine and God will be pleased!

River of Life Church

As I was seeking employment elsewhere and leaving Born Again Church (which was one of the hardest things I had to do in my life), a wonderful pastor friend of mine was in need of a secretary. Pastor Johnny Minick was the pastor of River of Life Church. I was hired and joined his fellowship and did active work at my new church! John and I were so loved and honored there for our giftings. We had a wonderful time of fellowship and growth there! I sang at every opportunity I was granted. I developed new departments of art for the ministry. We became busy in the world of arts; I made sure of it. It's what God does. Where He plants you, you are intended to grow. This is God's design for your life. God planted us there and we grew, even though my Black Gospel sound became offensive to some; as one lady told me when I got off stage from leading worship, "Come here Sis. Angie. I saw you up there shaking your tail feathers. If I had wanted to watch *Soul Train*, I would have stayed at home." My feelings were hurt just a little, but I couldn't help but laugh at her nerve in telling me!

Oh, my sweet Pastor Johnny and his wife Sherry went through trials keeping us encouraged in a Caucasian church that didn't understand my way of worship. My husband asked me if I saw a sister praying against me every time I got up to lead worship. It was said that because I had introduced the drama ministry to the church, I was doing nothing but acting out worship! Oh, but I had a cussing pastor in the pulpit whose name was Uncle Roger! Y'all, he was hilarious! He didn't allow anything to go unsaid about us. He protected us with his life, and everyone knew: don't bring him no foolish reports about nothing, especially us! He would say, "Don't bring me nothing you ain't ready to carry back!" He would say things like this all the time, amongst other choice words. But his love for John and me was real!

White Skinned Legs!
My husband had a bad fire accident that burnt both legs from the knees down with third degree burns. It was really bad. Our administrator Pastor Darrell, aka "Pastor D," came to visit us in the hospital and said that the men at the church heard that John was needing skin for his skin grafting surgery and they had decided to donate their skin. Y'all—this was an "all-white" church! LOL! As much pain as John was in, he couldn't help but holler and laugh and decline the offer! Even in opposition, God granted us favor so that we were able to navigate around all negativity. God is yet directing our path!

Lynda Randle

I received a call from a singer whose singing sessions we had done in the past; her name is Lynda Randle. She wanted to know if Gale and I would be willing to do some road dates with her. Of course; this is what we do! Bill Gaither had paired us together on videos in the past and it was always successful, so Lynda decided to take it on the road, and she did!

While being her singer, the administrator in me noticed that she needed assistance in her office. She not only hired us to sing, but Gale and I were hired as her staff members. We worked out of our homes for her for about 5 years while traveling to Kansas monthly for staff meetings. One day, she asked us why we didn't have any recordings of ourselves since we have sung for others for years. Well, to us, there was no need to have recordings of our own; we were background vocalists. She insisted that we become the artists we were called to be! My question was, *A recording for what? I was happy being a BGV!* She encouraged us and suggested something unheard of. She told us if we recorded, she would allow us room on her product table to sell it. *What?! You would share your product table? Unheard of in Black Gospel music.*

Gale and I were blessed with another stream of income. Look at God at work. He knew I would frown on the idea of a recording to be an artist. I had seen *sooo* many disappointing things in the field of Gospel music and I did not ever want to become a part of this or its necessity to be heard. He cleverly presented it as another stream of income for me to obey His calling on my life and record. God had it already set up for me. Gale and I had been recording for a Disney songwriter and he offered me his studio for free!

(Lord have mercy!!!) Did you hear me say *free?!* And this offer came with his engineer. Here was birthed my debut recording, "A Little Bit of Heaven." Lynda loved it and encouraged me to walk on water! She still encourages everything I do to this day. She is my sister forever!

Closed Door – Open Window

Lynda's dates began to allow a budget for her only and not her entire team. I saw the writing on the wall, and when the writer of "We Are Standing on Holy Ground," Geron Davis, asked if I could do some dates with him, I jumped on the opportunity. Can you see God at work? Your life is a pathway paved by God! As He lays the paver down—walk upon it!

Daddy Gee

Geron Davis, affectionately known as my "Daddy Gee," spoiled me on the road! He wouldn't allow me to pick up a suitcase. I wasn't used to this type treatment. The road motto is: "Don't bring what you can't carry." The only thing his wife and I had to do were get our singing parts correct. Every note is orchestrated by him, and he knows when you're slacking and doesn't mind telling you to pick up your pace. I would tell him, "Daddy Gee, I hear it this way." *(He's famous for telling you to do it the way you hear it on your record! LOL!)* Becky (his wife) and I would laugh all the time because we couldn't sneak anything past him. I mean *nothing!* Even when he was correcting charts or teaching a one-hundred voice choir, he would still hear what we sang wrong, weren't singing right, or not singing at all!

Geron is never too busy to hear the correctness in music. He could be in deep conversation in another part of the room, but if you've hummed it, he heard it! I couldn't believe his ears to hear *everything!* What is to be sung is in his head, and that's what he wants to hear! As adamant as he is to take care of you, he is just that adamant about his music.

Even when Geron appears to be sitting still, he really isn't. He is writing a song or arranging music in his head. Then he will teach you the parts to the song he just wrote—on the way to the venue. Our rides to the singing engagements were rehearsals. We never knew what to expect because his mind *never* stops. If he heard it, he wrote it, and we sang it!

A lady could never feel safer than under his care. He took care of me and everything concerning me. I love having Daddy Gee in my musical journey!

There are *sooo* many producers and singers in Nashville and the surrounding areas who have hired my services and I'm sooo grateful. If not for them, my career would be simply empty and nonexistent. It would be impossible for me to name all the producers God has blessed me with, because there are hundreds of them. If I were to take the time to research all my calls and producers, this book could easily be to me the yellow pages of Nashville's studios and producers.

However, there are stories of those who have made pivotal transitions in my life that warrants mentioning, and these stories could possibly help you. I want you to learn!

For 34 years, God has blessed me with this career of singing and it would not have been possible without the favor of God and man. Thank you for loving and calling me!

New Sponsor, My White Mommy

On my first date singing with Bill Gaither, I had a lady—may I say a little, sweet white lady—approach my table and express sadness because I only had one CD. I was looking at her strangely because I was grateful for the one I had! She kept asking, "Darlin' is this all you have?" Now I am asking myself, *"What's wrong with her? Isn't this all she sees, and why is she asking this?"* She stood back against the wall opposite of my table and watched me engage with my buying audience—my one CD. That following week I received a phone call from this lady. She spoke so sweetly and concerned as to why I only had one. I explained that budgeting is an issue as well as how much it costs to produce and manufacture new materials.

From that day to this one, 7 CDs later, she contributes more than 50% of my recording budgets. Is she a millionaire? No; she works night shifts at Walmart and is over 70 years of age. Eleven Kinkade paintings, 20 Brahmin bags, and diamond bracelets later, she yet gives! This is the Favor of God at its most magnificent.

Facebook Favor

I had someone read a FB post about me trying to complete my Mahalia Jackson CD and that I was lacking funds. They called to confirm and mailed me a check for $5,000.00. This woman had never met me in her life! She felt the need to support the sound of traditional Black Gospel music through me, and may I say she is white. I was *sooo* humbled, and still am! She continues to check on my progress and asks if there is anything she can do. Since her initial check, she has supported other projects of mine with her finances. I'm sooo grateful. It's something I can't explain. It just happens when your purpose and obedience is to walk in faith and God's favor.

With this same Mahalia Jackson project, another artist heard of my plight and needing help with my budget. My producer spoke with him and explained all that was needed to make it happen and that the budget had been expended. This artist listened with a giving heart and immediately called his office and they forwarded me a check for $5,000.00!

There have been other singers who understand the struggle of getting things done and have given to me via money apps with a note attached simply saying, "I'm loving you today! Be Blessed!" This is what God means when He says He will give you favor with great men!

I have an anonymous realtor who blesses ministries that are laid on her heart via prayer. I have gotten emails stating, "You've Got Money!" and it would be her sending sometimes $1,200.00. I've never met her, but connected to her through Facebook. I'm *sooo* grateful!!!

It's amazing what God does and who He uses. Never underestimate the workings of God. He is able!

Little Big Sister Sara from Mexico

I was singing in North Carolina at a praise gathering and this lady walked over to me and handed me a donation. I didn't open the check until that evening when counting the cash box and noticed the check was for $500.00. Well, I'm thinking this is a mistake; surely, she meant to write $50.00 or even $5.00, not $500! I called the number on the check and she answered and I told her of her mistake and that I would be at the church in the morning to return it to her. She told me that it wasn't a mistake and that it was my offering from her. *What?!* And she has been giving to this ministry ever since. She reads my website to see when I'm traveling next and always forwards via CashApp or Paypal $50 for coffee or a steak on my trip. Who thinks like this?! Who is this thoughtful? On a fixed income, she is. These are acts only God can do and orchestrate for you!

Everything That Glitters Ain't Gold

I've spoken a lot about giving, as this is what God requires of us. We are born to be givers. According to the Gospel book of Mark, Jesus was bombarded by those who were sick and needed healing and deliverance. In one passage, they had witnessed His gift the day before and came the next day asking for Him to do the same thing again. They were in need of His gift. The disciples were informed of the crowd waiting and asking of Him. Jesus responds in Mark 1:38 (TPT), *"We have to go on to the surrounding villages so that I can give My message to the people there, for that is My mission."* Jesus understood their plight, and He also understood His purpose and why He came!

We oftentimes get comfortable with what works and forget about furthering our purpose. You must ask yourself continuously, "Why am I here?" This is a question that your gift can't answer for. You are more than your gift! Be purpose-driven and not gift-persuaded. Your gift is to follow your purpose as opposed to your purpose following your gift. You must discover who you are and why you are here. Your gift is empty without purpose! Purpose develops legacy. Legacy tells others, "why you came."

Your gift is only part of your story! When your purpose is flighty with uncertainties, you become prey to satan. It is said that the graveyard is full of potential. It is full of people who never lived out their purpose, therefore, missing their potential. Seek God for your own purpose in life and live by His instruction with the gift He gave you. Don't commit to living someone else's life; I don't care how glamorous it seems to be. Everything that glitters ain't gold. God has His own plan for your life. He isn't short of ideas for you and your gift.

Don't settle for the gift seeker; settle for the gift maker! There are talent scouts and talent scalps! There are people who can help you and there are those who will scalp you! The enemy has representatives out there who will sell you and your gift to the highest bidder. They will promise you gold when in reality it's only gold plated. They will use your gift for their gain and leave you compromised and face down in sin's filthy dirt.

Success, accomplishment, and fame are often cloaked in cloths of shame. Don't fall for it. Recognize compromise by studying the Word of God and praying. Understand that the gold paint of compromise will eventually lose its color and reveal its true identity. When compromise is attached to it, it is not God. His purpose comes without temptation. If it ain't godly, then it ain't God! I've seen this so many times when viewing a television series, titled *Unsung*. Some of these people give their all to be famous to only be noted as "Un." *Think about it.*

CONCLUSION

God will lead you. His blessings are without sorrow. You may ask, "How can a good thing not be God?" The answer is: everything that is good is not of God, or should I say is not expedient. The devil has a way of presenting himself as an angel of light, but he isn't. We can't get caught up on what we think God wants and what is ideal for our lives. We have to seek Him daily to know what His ideal is. This information only comes through prayer. Yes, we will often miss it, but God has a way of honoring our desire to please Him and He can even make our mistakes prosper.

Find a prayer group to join. Find interactive work-books in the areas that God is leading you. You can find everything on Amazon! We no longer have excuses for not obtaining resources for our purpose and journey. Search autobiographies of kindred souls, people you consider he-roes of the gospel, and study their strengths and weaknesses. Study traits to embrace or rebuke.

Don't confuse the applause of man with the applause of God. To the carnal ear, they can sound identical, but the spiritual ear will convict you to righteousness. Remember that God applauds what comes from the inside, and man applauds what is seen on the outside. Man will give you 15 minutes of stardom and when you no longer bring them the goods, they no longer have use for you or your gift. God will promote you throughout eternity and He never forgets you! Your portrait will always hang on His wall of fame and will never collect dust!

Nothing I have achieved or am has been attained by conventional means. Everything I have accomplished in life has been the result of divine intervention. Everything!!!

So...You Say You Want to Sing. Who do you want to sing for? Why are you singing? Why are you even gifted to sing? What are you honestly seeking to accomplish with your gift of singing? Whose promotion do you really desire? Are you willing to get in the ranks with God or will you be satisfied only pleasing man? Understand this: the two will never mix! Are you seeking earthly or Heavenly gain? Earthly gain will be burned, while Heavenly gain is being stored up for you in Heaven.

Which will it be for you?
How will your story unfold?
Let's see...